Conspiracy
in the Town
that Time Forgot

CONSPIRACY IN THE TOWN THAT TIME FORGOT

Conspiracy in the Town that Time Forgot

Based on a true story

Stan St. Clair
with
Ron Cunningham

Edited by Michele Doucette

ISBN 978-0-9801704-9-8

Printed in the United States of America by
St. Clair Publications
P. O. Box 726
Mc Minnville, TN 37111-0726

http://stan.stclair.net

Cover photo property of Ron Cunningham.
Previously used by Jack Daniel Distillery
in their ad in Rolling Stone Magazine

Table of Contents

Ron Cunningham, while Sheriff of Moore County, receiving a plaque distinguishing him as a lifetime member of the Tennessee Sheriff's Association Youth Town Builder's Club. -Photo property of Ron Cunningham

Introduction and Credits

Ronald Reagan Cunningham was born in Coffee County, Tennessee on Wednesday August 8, 1945 to Roy E. and Louthine Todd Cunningham. Named by an uncle and aunt after the movie star who would later become the fortieth US President, he was born at home on Shelbyville Highway near the Moore-Bedford County line.

The Cunningham family moved around a lot during the time he was growing up. Ron had to be alone a great deal of the time because of his mother's frequent hospitalizations, often in Nashville. Ron was given to other families to keep on several occasions. His older sister helped out whenever possible. Because of these extenuating circumstances, Ron joined the Navy in 1963, at age seventeen. After a few transfers, he was sent to Norfolk, Virginia, and given service aboard three ships. He describes it as "seeing the world through a porthole". Finally he was transferred to Philadelphia.

During this tour of duty, he married Linda Dale Hudson of the Pleasant Hill Community of Moore County, Tennessee. Their first child, Shannon Marie, was born at Philadelphia Naval Hospital. From there, he went back to Norfolk, where he had knee surgery due to an injury. There, their second daughter, Leah Dawn, was born. In 1972, he was honorably discharged, but stayed in their Virginia home until July of 1974. On a two week vacation to visit Linda's parents in Moore County, as Linda and her mother were about to leave on a shopping trip, Ron jokingly told them that if he could get a job before they returned, they would move back to Tennessee. They had hardly gotten out of sight when Sheriff Chuck Johnson knocked on the door. As it was election year, the sheriff was soliciting votes. Ron asked Chuck if he needed a deputy, and he responded in the affirmative, but told him that he would have to talk to the county judge. Ron and the judge were immediately compatible. He told Ron that the job was his providing it was Okayed by the County Commissioners. After returning to his in-laws' home, the judge called and gave him the thumbs up.

When Linda and her mother returned from shopping in Tullahoma, they could not believe his startling news.

Ron's early life experiences, coupled with his stint in the Navy, prepared him to view his position in law enforcement as a very serious calling. He served as deputy until 1976, when he was first elected sheriff. He believes that crimes are serious and deserve serious consequences. His stance won him friends among decent, law-abiding people, but conversely, he was despised by those whom he punished, as well as by their families. So much so, that at least two wished him dead, and came very nearly to accomplishing their goal. This is that shocking true story. Some names have been changed to protect the innocent.

In 1974, while living in Lynchburg, a third daughter, Yolanda, was born to the Cunninghams.

I wish to thank Ron for choosing me to relate his remarkable story in more vivid detail than ever before. I also want to give credit to Ron's wife, Linda, whose talented work has been utilized to a great degree, especially in the genesis of this book. And I wish to express my thanks to all those who reported these events, or worked on this material to help make the story fit together more smoothly. Thanks also are due to Lester Brown, brother of the late Lacy "Moon" Brown, for giving me permission to use material which was to be used for the television movie about this case, in the writing of this book. And finally, many thanks go to my dear friend, Nate Wolf, for directing me to pertinent facts which facilitated in the betterment of deriving the more complex nature of this case. Several original documents and transcripts have been utilized in the authentic recreation of this dramatic true story, in an effort to keep it as nearly accurate as possible. This saga involves a number of very well-known individuals, including the ex-governor of Tennessee. In much the same way that information obtained by Clifford Irving in the writing of the unauthorized "Autobiography of Howard Hughes" in 1971 led to the Watergate break in, and the eventual downfall of President Richard M. Nixon, information given to the agents in the case of Ron Cunningham aided in the demise of the political career of ex-Governor Ray Blanton. At the time, in early 1979, parts of this dramatic ordeal made national and international headlines, and offers poured in for book and movie rights. For personal and legal reasons, these were rejected. The time has finally come to tell all. It is Ron's wish that profanity be eliminated.

Chapter One

The early July heat hung heavily over the small southern town of Lynchburg. The solitary sign of life, from the vantage point of the town square, was an observant hawk, lazily riding the air currents as if he had nothing better to do. A few hours earlier the square had been a beehive of activity, with curious tourists from around the globe, drawn there by the world-famous Jack Daniel Distillery, and the quaint hamlet that time seemed to have passed over. But now, in the scorching afternoon, the square was deserted. All of the tourists had sought refuge from the heat in the air-conditioned motels in nearby towns. A commercial had just been filmed there for national television staring two legendary figures: the great Johnny Cash and the incomparable race car driver, Richard Petty. Two other men in Lynchburg that day were very impressed with the simple Mayberry-like quality that they felt. One was a visitor. The other, the sheriff, had but a few years before, returned from his tour of military service. The cunning visitor toured the distillery, and roamed in and out of the cozy little shops which encircled the square. In its center stood a stately 1880's era red brick courthouse with white-columned porches. These two men, unknown to each other, would soon be on a collision course which could prove deadly to one of them.

The visitor, known as Rivers, had come from Michigan. A felon, recently released from prison, he could hardly contain the excitement he felt at his discovery. *Imagine*, he thought, *a real Mayberry RFD, complete with simple country folk! And what's really important, a country bumpkin for a sheriff!* Since his release, he couldn't chance staying in Michigan: there was too much danger there for business-as-usual. But this - this place was perfect! A store on, or perhaps just off, this charming square, catering to tourists hungry for country curios and / or memorabilia would be the ideal cover for his illegal operations. He would be returning to Michigan in a few days, but he would certainly be back. Just as soon as he wrapped up a few business deals already in the making, he and his wife, Nona, would move there. Rivers chuckled to himself as his tires hummed down highway 55 toward the Interstate which would connect the Southeastern states to those in the North. He could just imagine his very northern wife joining the quilting guild he'd seen advertised on a flyer in the White Rabbit.

The White Rabbit Saloon, situated on the east side of the square, looked as if it might have been relocated from Dodge City, Kansas. Built in the late 1880's, it had once been not only a thriving saloon, but also a well-known gambling house. However, its days as such an establishment had come to a screeching halt when the state legislature made the entire state dry in 1912. Almost seventy years later, very little had changed here. The huge solid mahogany bar ran almost the entire length of the interior of what had been the saloon. Behind it, the original full-wall mirror was still in tact. The bar, complete with a brass foot rail and spittoon, now used as a deli, was very popular with both tourists and locals. Overhead, a long rod supported fans which turned slowly, creating a faint breeze as the second man, the sheriff of Moore County, sat pensively at the far end of the bar, nursing a root beer.

"Need another one, Sheriff?'

"No, don't think so, Jake. I need to get back over to the jail."

"By the way, did I hear that you came down pretty hard on Earl James's boy this week?

"You're darn right I did, and I'll do it again if he doesn't get the message! I'm not putting up with that boy's crap! "

"I may be speaking out of turn, Sheriff, but even if you are from around here, you've been away for a long time. Things change. This county's not the same as it was when you left."

"That's a bunch of crap, Jake; right is right, and wrong is wrong. That doesn't change."

"I hear you, Sheriff, but there's been a lot of new people coming in here, and they ain't all good. That James is one of 'em. Don't know who he is, or where he's from, but I'm here to tell you, he's not one to mess with."

"I don't give a rat's tail who he is, if that boy breaks the law I'm going after him. Shoot, Jake, that wasn't just some teenage prank he pulled, and I don't intend to let him get away with it!"

"What did the boy do, anyway?"

"The first time I arrested him, he threw a bag out of his car out near the high school with a pound of marijuana in it. I had him hands down. They let him off on that before, when I was Chief Deputy. This time he was destroying personal property. I've just had enough!"

"I know you've had your problems with the court. Didn't you have some other things dismissed as deputy?"

21

"Stinking right I did! Remember when I found that stuff under those bridges?"

"Seems like it. What exactly happened?"

"Well, one day I was having breakfast with Chuck and the State Trooper at City Café, and they told me that the Co-op had been broken into over the weekend. They both wanted me to do the investigation. I went over and took a bunch of pictures, and fingerprinted the place. Well alright, now I thought things went really well, because a couple of days later, I was out close to the school on 55, and saw a couple of young fellows go under the bridge. They didn't stay under there but just a bit, and went back up to the high school. Well, naturally, I went under that bridge to find out what the Sam Hill they had done down there, and lo and behold, there was a clear plastic bag in the creek with a bunch of knives in it. I put it back where I found it, and that afternoon after school, I hid and saw those same two boys go back under the bridge and pull the bag out and leave with it. I followed them, and arrested them, recovering the property which had been stolen. Guess what. The dang charges were dismissed."

Jake chuckled nervously.

"Then I was called and told that a house had been broken into. 'They took my collection of knives, old guns and watches,' the guy told me. I saw some boys going under the bridge out on Hwy 50 the next day. Later, I went under that bridge, and up on a ledge I found the items stolen from that house. Guess what. It was the same two boys who stole the stuff from the Co-op. And, you guessed it. They dropped the charges again!"

"Well, Sheriff, I certainly know what you mean. You know that most folk around here support what you're doing, but there are some who don't. And obviously, the families who are involved have more pull than you. And this is election year. I think you're trying to be like that sheriff up in west Tennessee, you know, Buford Pusser. He was real tough, or thought he was. You know where that got him...dead!"

"Don't you think you're exaggerating a little?"

"No, Sheriff, I'm just trying to tell you that you better watch your butt!"

Chapter Two

The bustling summer months had seemed to evaporate as a steamy vapor. The 1978 sheriff election proved the fact that the good citizens of Moore County still had not lost their voice. Ron had stayed busy on the campaign trail, and had won his post back handily.

But there had been a few quirky incidents involving marijuana, in which Ron had been required to think fast. For one, while sitting in the jail, he had spotted a hippy-type across the street, near the courthouse, who appeared to be jerking on a joint. When he approached, in uniform, the young long-hair made no attempt to hide the joint.

"Hey, man, whatcha doin'?" Ron said.

"Smokin' weed, man."

"You got any more of that stuff?"

"Sure. I got some here in the glove compartment of my car. Ya want some?"

"Well, is that all you have?"

"No, man! I got plenty. Here," he said, raising the trunk lid, "I've got several kilos in here. We have lots of this stuff out at the Farm."

Ron was extremely familiar with the "Farm", a notorious compound in a nearby county.

"Hey, dude, I'm the sheriff here in Moore County, Ron Cunningham."

The stoned man reached out his hand and smiled. "Hey, Sheriff, glad to meet you!"

"You're under arrest, my man, for possession of controlled substance with intent to resell. Anything you say can and will be used against you in..,"

"Hey, Sheriff! Wait a dern minute! Do you remember when God appeared to Moses in a burning bush?"

"I've heard the story. What's that got to do with anything?"

"Well, God appeared to me in a marijuana bush and told me that it was alright to smoke this stuff. God is superior to your law!"

"Hey, God told me to uphold the law of the land, and you're still under arrest!"

"I get a phone call!"

The call was to his lawyer, who backed the story of his client, claiming divine right to smoke whatever he chose. Ron was never shocked at the brass that people had. He even had run-ins with members of important political families, one of whom was blatantly dragging on a joint. For sure, inhaling.

Another incident that summer had involved a helicopter flight to arrest local growers. The pot patch had been spotted by the regional ATF agent who, along with Ron, utilized an ex-sheriff of a neighboring county.

The chopper hummed in, the blades echoing their deafening song. As it neared the surface of the hillside, the agent yelled, "Jump!"

Ron landed, sprawling headlong on one of the fleeing suspects. What an adventure. But it was a successful one. A bit of a sprained ankle was no deterrent to the capture. The growers were jailed and the crop chopped.

◆◆◆

October had now rushed in, and the presence of autumn had given a brisk chill to the wholesome rural air. The bright reds of the sourwoods, mingled with the yellow poplars and varied shades of maple, were already being carried by the gentle breezes which drifted lazily through the ancient valley.

A meeting that month was about to change history.

"Clinton Rivers? I'm Earl James. I hear that you're new in Lynchburg, and you've opened

29

this strip mall here." Rivers was getting ready to answer, but James continued, "I haven't been around Moore County long either. We came a few months ago from Florida. Where'd you folks come from?" James removed his faded Jack Daniel cap, and pushed his way into the store, glancing with curiosity at the packed displays.

The small strip mall was located just out of the main part of town, but close enough in for easy access to the center of "Mayberry".

"Yeah, I'm Rivers. We blew in from up north during the summer, Michigan, to be exact. Nona's settin' some more stuff up. She's my better half."

"Hey, Miz Nona. How are you doin'?"

Nona merely nodded and continued her preoccupation with her work getting organized. But she was forever listening. She brushed the uninvited visitor, and picked up a price tag which he had inadvertently knocked over. As would soon become obvious to Earl James, Nona was a major player in all of her husband's operations.

Out of the corner of his eye, Rivers spotted the sheriff directly across the street. He knew that Ron wouldn't be hanging out around there for any reason other than to try to determine what he was up to. It was painfully easy for him to tell that this unorthodox lawman had been tipped off, and was keeping a close watch on every twitch of so little as one of his pinkies.

"What do you think of Sheriff Cunningham, James? I hear he's kind of a rough character."

Earl James' face went ashen. "I'm sorry, man," he said, almost choking and wagging his head slowly, "but you've just hit the worst possible nerve in me! That SOB is achin' for a breakin'!"

"Gees, I didn't mean get you *all shook up.*" Rivers twisted his hip and acted like Elvis. "What's your beef with the good sheriff?"

"Good sheriff, the dickens! That freakin' man is Satan himself. He's been known to beat folks with a ball bat, I understand, and he's taken his spite out on my son for the last freakin' time."

"Well, I've got to admit I don't think much of him myself."

"I'm not surprised. If you're not from around here, and don't think like him, he's likely to get it in for you."

A warm friendship began to take root between the two bitter newcomers, and they would often spend an entire afternoon just hanging out, or would cheerfully chat while sipping their morning cups of steaming java. Soon they were discussing moving a variety of stolen goods like guns, boats, and bulldozers. James shared his expertise about heavy equipment, and the like, while Clinton and Nona explained their knowledge of the illegal gun trade.

♦ ♦ ♦

Lacy "Moon" Brown was one of the most renowned special agents of his day, whose story ended up in places like Playboy, Field and Stream, and the Detroit Free Press Magazines. After serving in the Marines, he had joined the Narcotics Division of the Flint Police Department, where he worked undercover. At this time he was with the Lapeer County, Michigan Sheriff's office. Because of his notoriety, however, Brown used other aliases when dealing with his suspects. He had met Clinton Rivers in Michigan while working undercover with another suspect. He had been introduced to Rivers as simply "Leonard from Port Huron". The two had hit it off remarkably well, and parlayed at great length about their common interest in both stolen goods and deer hunting. Rivers had told him of his plans to come up to go hunting at the beginning of the next deer season. This would be an ideal way to get their partnership moving. Moon had given him information about a rustic cabin in the Upper Peninsula. He had jotted down Rivers' number and had told him that he would be in touch regarding some new guns which he hoped to soon acquire.

◆ ◆ ◆

A number of calls between Moon and Rivers were made in which they had discussed a partnership in obtaining a large quantity of new stolen handguns which had been offered to Rivers. By dividing them, Rivers felt more confident that they could arrange a wider range of distribution, thus making detection by the authorities less likely.

On the morning of Tuesday, November 14th, after a failed attempt to contact him while he was visiting his wife in the hospital, Moon again rang Rivers' office.

"C and N Plaza," a female voice said.

"Yes, could I speak to the Rivers?"

"Okay, just a second. Hey! Rivers, you're wanted on the phone!"

"Thanks, I've got it back here. Hello."

"Port Huron Leonard here, dude, what's happ'nin'?"

"Oh, nothin' right now."

"How's the wife? She get out? I heard she was in the hospital."

"No, not yet. She'll be out in the mornin', probably."

"You ain't gonna make openin' day either, huh?"

"Nope."

"I say 'either', 'cause I'm not gonna get to make it up right now. I've got some runnin' to do. I won't be up, probably, till tomorrow night. You think you'll be up before the season's over?"

"Oh, sure. Wouldn't miss it."

"Okay, get somethin' to write with and I'll give you the number where I'm gonna be at."

"Okay."

"I'll be at 616-555-1414, and if I'm not there, leave a message with Big Ed, but nobody else, 'cause he's the guy that sees after the deer hunters and stuff around up there. And I don't know who might answer the phone. Ed'll know where I'll be. Like if I'm out, or somethin'."

"Alrightee."

"Well, so, how's things goin'?"

"Oh, pretty good. It don't do no good to complain, ya know."

"Ain't that the truth! What about us buying the new ones? You know. The ones you were lookin' at. "

"If we get the new ones, you'll need to take care of the serial numbers."

"I don't understand, Rivers."

"Well, see, they would have to go through the store."

"Oh, through your store down there? Well, that won't involve me none up here, right?"

"Well. Somebody's gotta get 'em fixed."

"Yeah, dude, you know I don't want nothin' to do with that. You get that handled. I don't care how, so long as I'm not involved."

"Right. I guess I can come up with somebody to do it."

"Hey, I'm goin' up tomorrow night. I've got a cold. But nothin' serious. If you bring your wife, though, keep her away from people, 'cause there's a lot of flu or something goin' around."

"Thanks for tellin' me, but she's not comin' anyway."

"Hey, I think traffic will be too heavy tomorrow morning, so I'm waitin' till tomorrow night to go up. I'm supposed to meet a friend of mine there. I'm planning on goin' over some prices with him, and see if he can't handle a couple of 'em. So, have you got any idea of when you might get there?"

"No, not sure till the wife gets home."

"Hey, what's wrong with her, anyway?"

"Aw, I think it's nerves more then anything. They're trying to get her blood pressure regulated."

"That blood pressure's bad business. My dad was havin' a hard time with his, and he had a stroke and has been in a wheelchair for about six years. He's in his fifties. So we're talkin' the new pieces. I figure I can handle about six Magnums right now, if you've already got a few on hand. I'll know more as soon as I talk to my man I'm gonna meet at the huntin' shack up there. You think she might get out tomorrow?"

"I hope so. And I think I've got you covered on those Magnums."

"Sounds great. Okay, why don't you give me a call at the number I gave you tomorrow night and let me know when you're comin' up, and I'll meet you somewhere."

"You'll be in after dark?"

"Huh?"

"You'll be *gettin'* in there after dark?"

"Yeah. Let's say after 10:00 o'clock to be safe. It'll take a while goin' up I 75. I'm down in Flint now. I'm wrapping up with a dude here.

Haven't run into any reasonable prices on any other new stuff, have you?"

"I may come up with something."

"Uh-huh."

"This guy's checkin' on it right now."

"Hey, on them numbers you was talkin' about, just make sure there ain't no way they can trace them up this way."

"Yeah. I can find somebody to take care of it right. I was just hopin' you had some connections."

"Na, man. I don't want no part of that."

"I heard you on that, right."

"It'll take me a couple of weeks. If I can get the supply, I've got the demand. You know I'll need a day or two in advance to get the money together for a large order like that."

"We'll see what that guy comes up with."

"Okay, but you'll definitely be in before Monday, right?

"I wantta be, yes."

"Don't worry about what time you get in even if it's 3:00 or 4:00 in the morning. Shoot, wakin' up don't bother me."

"Alrightee."

"Hey, I just want to get some bucks rollin' in. Okey dokey?"

"I can use that, too ."

"Okey dokey. You sound like my man. I'll catch you later."

"Okay. Bye bye."

"Bye."

♦ ♦ ♦

"Look over on that little rise," Moon whispered, pointing at a picturesque buck. "What a beaut! You want a crack at him?"

"Go ahead, Lenny, you saw him first." Grey puffs rose from the nostrils of the gorgeous, stately twelve-pointer, and slowly faded into the frosty sky. Moon's 30.30 sounded through the early morning like a bolt of lightning crackling into the trunk of a massive oak. The shot struck its victim squarely in the heart. Rivers marveled at the accuracy of the hit, and the sheer beauty of the graceful fall.

"Man, you're good with that thing."

"I enjoy the sport, and I dearly love eatin' venison." Moon ran his fingers slowly through his ruffled beard, and a tinge of a smile began to form on his lips. He flung the shell from the rifle chamber, and wrapped his bulky mackinaw more tightly around his hefty waist.

"Same here, man." Rivers licked his dry, cold lips, and it seemed that his tongue would freeze immovably to them,

"I'll be glad to divvy up the meat with you."

"Thanks. I'll take you up on that, my friend."

"After we get him weighed in, there's a processing house right down the road where we can get it dressed and divided up. We'll just tell them to give us equal shares, and we can each pay our half when we pick it up.'

"My man! Will do."

The two burley men not only enjoyed the vigorous hunt, but were beginning to develop a sound personal relationship.

"I think we'll work really well together," Moon said with a naughty grin. "And, by the way, I've got us a sale for those six pieces right now, if you've got 'em with you."

Chapter Three

Thanksgiving Day was a welcome break for Ron from the tension-filled week. On the previous Tuesday he had been in court on a case in which a dispute, earlier that fall, between two farmers, had resulted in one taking the life of the other.

Their farms were adjoining along Highway 55. One day, as one was cutting his hay field, he ran his mower into the fence of his neighbor, a distant cousin of his wife. The other farmer, who had been observing from his porch, then made his way to the field.

"Don't you be running into my fence any more, Roy! Watch what you are doin'."

He was ignored. Roy was a large man, and the offended neighbor knew that he was not to be taken lightly if irritated. On the next round, the mower blades again struck the fence with a resounding thud.

.

By this time, the neighbor was getting even angrier, and when, on the third trip, the action was again repeated; he retrieved his shotgun, aimed it at the offender and pulled the trigger. The pellets entered the left arm, and lodged in big Roy's heart.

Fortunately, when Ron questioned the farmer, he came clean and was arrested without incident.

In addition, on Wednesday, Ron had just been through the hectic ordeal of feeling it necessary to fire a deputy. He had arrested two men who were playing loose with guns, and when he brought them in, the deputy was leisurely leaning against a mantle. While attempting to get the captives into the cells, one had almost escaped, and the deputy hadn't offered to lift a hand to help.

Now, with the holiday, Ron hoped for a slack in action. He opened the door, with a smile, to find his in-laws waiting to enter.

"Hey, Mom and Dad, how ya'll doin'? Linda's got dinner cooking. While y'all are visiting, I need to take a run out in the country and see how things are clicking. I'm going to take a little drive and try to relax a bit, if y'all don't mind."

"Of course not, Ron. We'll see you when you get back."

Ron breathed deeply as he cranked his cruiser and gradually made his way along the gravel lane toward the old Ledford Mill. *It would be so very relaxing,* he thought, *just to take a leisurely drive and let Linda and the girls visit with her parents awhile.* Peace and quiet certainly had been at a premium.

The day was near picture-perfect. The sky was a pristine blue, hardly lighter than had been October's notorious hue. Only a few cumulous clouds floated about the heavens.

What the...? Ron couldn't believe his eyes. A cowboy, or someone thinking himself to fit the bill, was standing by the road, next to an awesome waterfall, acting a bit tipsy. In his hand he held the reigns to his chestnut mare. Strangely enough, the animal was acting a little unusual as well. In the man's holsters were two whisky bottles, their necks pointed downward.

"Hey, fella," Ron said, "you been drinkin'?"

"Well," he drawled, I've had one little drink, but my horse has had two!"

As Ron was about to advise him to head his four-legged friend toward the corral, the cowboy jumped on the horse and took off in a gallop, repeatedly giving Ron the finger in a most unfriendly manner.

Though attempting to stay with him for safety sake, Ron had soon lost the uncouth horseman.

"Ma'am," Ron said to a lady at a nearby house, "I seem to have misplaced a cowboy who has had a little too much holiday spirits. Do you happen to know where I could find somebody like that around these parts?"

"Yes sir, that there would be ol' Joe Bandy. He lives just up the road, third house on the left. Can't miss it. There's a big barn right there next to it. And a horse lot. He just has the one horse."

"Thank you very much, ma'am. Have a nice Thanksgiving." Ron tipped his hat, and backed away.

Soon it was evident which place was Joe's.

"Hello, ma'am. I'm Sheriff Cunningham..."

"'Course you are! I know who you are! Doesn't everybody in Moore County?" I saw your picture on every tree and road sign durin' the election. Won't you come in?"

"Thank you, but I'm looking for Joe Bandy. Would he happen to be your husband?"

"Dang right he is, and he's right in there at the kitchen table! He's drunk as a skunk again, and I can't keep him from actin' stupid sometimes. Just take him on to jail. I don't want him around here when he's been on the sauce."

"Joe, I didn't come here to take you to jail," Ron said most apologetically. "You've got a barn out there. Do you have some hay in one of the stalls, or maybe in the loft?"

"Why sure, what's it to ya?"

"Now, Joe, you need to go out there and sleep it off. I don't want to take you to jail. You were acting a little wild out there."

"Well, I'd rather sleep with my horse than my old lady, anyway. At least she treats me good."

"Now, Joe, that's your only choice. Will you promise me you'll go out there and sleep this off?"

"I'll go."

"You folks have yourselves a real nice Thanksgiving."

Ron rolled his eyes and shook his head on the way to the car. He cranked his cruiser, backed out of the drive and headed home to join his family for a fine dinner of turkey and all of the trimmings. He had had enough excitement for a Thanksgiving Day. In spite of all of the problems, he felt that he had much for which to be thankful.

Chapter Four

Meanwhile, the friendship was continuing to blossom between Rivers and James. They had formed a tight partnership in dealing with the goods being brought in from Michigan. As they were lifting a toast to their camaraderie that Christmas Eve, James spoke up.

"We're about the same age, Rivers, and we think a lot alike. We might be able to be of a help to each other in more than one way. We're starting to work well together in the business."

"Yeah, talk on."

"You know what Cunningham is puttin' both of us through. We can't turn our backs for one darn minute but what he's lookin' over our shoulders. Why don't you just knock him off?"

"Me? I can't do somethin' like that! There has to be another way to get him off our backs besides killin' him, right? That sounds a little desperate."

"Hey man, I guess I'm just thinkin' out loud. That guy's just gettin' under our skin. I'm afraid it's gonna end up either him or one of us."

"I just know I don't want anything to do with takin' anybody out. Especially a lawman."

Well, if you don't do it, I'll have to find another way to get him taken care of, if I have to do it myself. Or there's some guy down in Huntsville who does stuff like that cheap. Five hundred, they say."

"Hey, man. You're talkin' crazy! And I've heard about that guy in Huntsville. You sure as heck don't want him. He's bad news. He's already been up the creek for a lot of stuff, and the law watches him like a freakin' hawk. He's liable to do a butcher job, and get caught, and sing like a canary."

"Hmm, when are you going back to Michigan?"

"Ah, I'm plannin' on a trip in January."

"I tell you what, when you go back up north next month, how about putting some feelers out for somebody who might be willing to help us get rid of our little sheriff problem. It'll probably be better if we find some guy from out-of-state, don't you think? I'll ante in for the hit if you get it lined up. Just tell me how much."

Nona nodded. She had warmed up to James and seemed grateful for his input. "I agree with Earl. We've got to do something. But I just hate to see it come to this. What if somethin' goes wrong?"

"If we're gonna stick our necks out, that's just a chance I'm afraid we're gonna have to take. We'll just have to be dang cautious who we deal with. I'll see what I can do."

◆ ◆ ◆

The frequent calls from Moon to Rivers continued, but the one placed on Tuesday, January 2nd, was to set the stage for the climactic plan which would lead to Rivers' downfall and the assumed hit on the sheriff of Moore County.

"I'm comin' north," Rivers said.

"Are you?"

"Yep!"

"Fantastic, when are you comin' up?"

"I'm supposed to leave here Thursday morning."

"Thursday morning. So that'll put you up here…"

"Thursday night,"

"Great. We can get together Thursday night, huh?"

"Let's try."

"Okay. What's the best number to reach you when you get in?"

"Ah, probably the boy's house there, Greg's"

"Greg's?"

"Yeah."

"See if I got it right...235-555-6611, right? I wrote it down when you gave it to me up at the cabin."

"Right."

"Okey-dokey! I got 'er then. Do you think about 9:00 or 10:00?"

"Yeah, that should be fine, I'm gonna fly, anyway."

I'll try to get a few bucks together. I was thinkin' about makin' a run down to Carolina to see my folks later anyway. They're from around Greensboro, and if I come up with somethin', and if I can spare a few days extra when I go down, maybe we can get together again then."

"Okay."

"Sound good?"

"Yep."

"Okay, see you later, Bud. Hey, did you have a nice Christmas and New Year?"

"Oh, yes!"

"Fantastic. Mama gettin' along Okay?"

"Oh, pretty good."

"Pretty good? Okay, so I'll see you Thursday night, then."

"Okay."

"Bye-bye."

◆ ◆ ◆

At 3:00 o'clock Thursday afternoon Moon hummed as he dialed the office to check on Rivers' progress.

"C and N," a male voice answered.

"Hey, how's it goin' buddy."

"Oh, not bad."

Obviously this isn't Rivers, he thought. "Ah, this is Port Huron Leonard. Did Rivers leave for Michigan yet?"

"Not yet."

"Not yet? Is he around?"

"Uh, I think so if he hasn't taken off any place. Hang on just a second."

"Sure."

"Hey, Rivers! That guy from Michigan is on the phone!"

"Lenny?"

"Rivers, how's it goin', buddy?"

"Well, just gettin' ready to leave."

"Oh, are you?"

"The only flight I could get was 6:45 tonight."

"Uh-oh!"

"So I'll be there at 11:00 tonight, and I'm stayin' all day tomorrow."

"Okay, so how about tomorrow. 'Cause I've gotta run. I drove down here tonight, and I've gotta meet some people about 10:00 in Port Huron."

"Uh-huh..."

"I'm down in Flint now. Maybe I didn't make that clear. Would tomorrow be good for you?"

"Yep."

"Okay, about what time?"

"Well, the only thing I've got goin' on tomorrow is a doctor's appointment at 3:00."

"Okay, how about around 6:00 or 7:00, somewhere in there?"

"Okay, at Greg's."

"Sounds good. And bring along some new catalogues. I'm ready to do some serious business."

♦ ♦ ♦

At their meeting late that Friday night, after browsing through his gun catalogue, Rivers' eyes took on a serious, almost glassy gaze. He had seen the accuracy at which his friend was able to bring down the mighty buck.

"I'm interested in doing this gun business with you, Lenny, but I've got another, even more pressing need. I want to have a man killed. Can you do it?"

Moon's brilliant instinct was rapid-fire. This sensational request had come out of left field and hit him squarely in the face. "Na, man, not me, I'll work with you on the guns and stuff like that all day, but that's not my bag. I know some people who might be willing do that kind of stuff, though."

"Yeah? That's great! When do I meet them?" Rivers' eyes widened and showed a ray of emerging hope.

"First I need to know who you want knocked off?"

It's a hick sheriff in Tennessee," Rivers said quietly, looking downward to avoid a possible backlash.

Moon's curious mind spun into high gear. *I wonder what the sheriff has done to him.* But he said merely, "Why do want him taken out?"

"Because, that son of a buck is causing me and this other guy some serious problems. He's messin' with our heavy equipment operations, and this other guy is really furious. This dog's replaced Buford Pusser, the way he's taking over everything."

Other guy? Moon thought. But his questions could wait.

"I'll talk to the people, and get you in touch with them if they're interested."

"Okay, dude. Let's see the pieces."

Rivers went to his car and opened the trunk. Moon was not disappointed; he had certainly come through. But now a different and much more alluring hand was in play. He could wait to lay his down.

"Thanks, man. These look great. I'll take 'em. You gonna have more of these soon?"

"Hope to. Gotta split. Catch ya later, dude."

As soon as he reached a pay phone, Moon reeled his car over. Rapidly, he dialed the number, "Shooter this is Moon. We have a big fish on the hook." Lacy Brown and Phil McCarty had worked together before. Now they could both feel it in their bones; they were about to pull in Moby Dick.

Chapter Five

"You're not gonna believe this, ma'am. I was driving out toward Tullahoma, in the country, and this...dadburn it! I don't need to be tellin' you this. Can I talk to the sheriff?" The caller was obviously highly perturbed.

"Sheriff Cunningham isn't here, sir, but I think I know what you are going to say. We've had a bunch of calls. Are you talking about a man exposing his hind parts?"

"Yes, ma'am. I can't believe anybody would be that crude and disrespectful. I had my wife with me in the car, and I was dang embarrassed, that's what I was. Can't the sheriff or one of his deputies do something to get this guy stopped from doin' this?"

"He's tried, sir. Several times. In fact one of the deputies has been out there, too. But they haven't seen hide nor hair of him. Get it? Hide nor hair! Ha, ha!"

"Ma'am, no disrespect, but this ain't a blamed bit funny! We're decent people. This is a disgrace to all of Moore County!"

"Yes, sir. We are doing all we can. I'll tell the sheriff you called. What time of day was it?"

"About 3:00 in the afternoon."

"Got it. 3:00 o'clock. Was that in Cumberland Springs area, right?"

"Yes 'am, on Cumberland Springs Road."

"I'll sure tell him you called."

♦ ♦ ♦

One early January evening while driving about, Ron did a double-take. *Could it be?* The weather was not conducive to exposure of one's tender parts. Spinning his cruiser around, he was soon parallel to the other vehicle. A huge, bare bottom was protruding from an open window.

I'll make sure this clown doesn't freeze his butt off, Ron thought. Reaching into the floorboard, he picked up a handgun which he had loaded with salt pellets, and fired it into the easy target, scoring a bull's eye. As he sped away, he chuckled. He could hear the resultant reaction for a good long while.

A little later, Ron happily whistled *Jingle Bells* as he drove to the nearest hospital emergency room in neighboring Tullahoma.

"Hi there. I'm Ron Cunningham, the sheriff from over in Lynchburg. Did you have a man come in not long ago with an injury to his back end?"

"Yes," the nurse said, frowning. "How did you know? Big guy?"

"Yeah, that's him. Well, I filled his sorry butt with salt for mooning me."

The nurse laughed so loudly that Ron wondered if the big fellow might have heard. "I'll teach him another lesson," she said, grinning.

Shortly, Ron could hear a repeat of the strange noises he had heard coming from the car on Cumberland Springs Road. For some reason, alcohol had not seemed to relieve his anguish.

The calls stopped reporting mooning. But Ron's real problems were just beginning.

Chapter Six

"C and N."

"Can I speak to Big Rivers?" Moon said.

"You got him."

"Hey, dude, you didn't sound like yourself! You must have the crud. I'm a little hoarse myself. How's the weather down your way?"

"Oh, it's cold."

"Cold, man? You don't know cold down there. It's so stinkin' cold up here that the windows are iced over on my car, and the doors are frozen shut. What you gonna be doin' about the 18th, 19th and 20th of January?"

"I'll be down here then."

"Okay. I'll slide your way about late the night of the 18th, me and my partner's gotta be down there anyway. We've got some pieces. And we were talkin' about groceries. Do you have any food stamps that way?"

"Yep."

"You interested in any?"

"Sure. Both pieces and stamps. We're always in the market when the price is right."

"Okay, 'cause we're gonna have some time when we come down. We'll probably have a few grand worth. You gonna have enough cash to handle 'em?"

"Yeah. If it's not too many grand."

"Fantastic! And on the rest, to have that little job done, my main man is comin' down and the price on that's somethin' you'll have to talk about to him, you know. He'll probably be down there about that time."

"He's interested?"

"Yeah, he's interested. But I don't want nothin' to do with that, you know. That would be between you and him. All I want out of it is a .44 Mag. And I never said who it was. That'll be up to you."

"Is he good?"

"Well, he'll be gettin' a man for you. He wants to talk to you before he turns you on to *his* man, you know. That'll be between you and him. I don't want any part of nothin' like that, but he's good, and knows the best, and he's also the dude that's got the stamps. You'll need just about two or three grand for those, I suppose"

"Alrightee, then. No problem."

"How far a drive is that from here?"

"635 miles."

"About how many hours?"

"About eleven and a half."

"I was thinkin' twelve."

"You can make it in eleven to eleven and a half without breakin' any speed laws. It's expressway all the way."

"Hey, I'll meet him down there. We'll be in town the same night. See you then, bud."

"Okay."

"Okey-dokey. Bye."

♦ ♦ ♦

Moon stretched and turned on his TV. It was Tuesday, January 16th, and the evening news was coming on.

"This just in: we have breaking news out of Nashville, Tennessee. Governor Ray Blanton left office three days early, paving the way for Lamar Alexander's swearing in today. An investigation

into allegations of charges that members of his staff were accepting pay for pardons is now officially underway. We do have word from a reliable source that before leaving office, a number of pardons of felons were signed by Governor Blanton. Stay tuned for further details..."

Moon shook his head. His life was devoted to uncovering information which aided in putting offenders behind bars, now a governor was apparently letting them go!

Chapter Seven

On the frigid afternoon of Friday, January 19th, 1979, Rivers and Nona met Vince and McCarty at the Sheraton Inn in East Ridge, just south of Chattanooga, at Moon's request. The clouds contained motley streaks of dark shades, and the breeze was one that could chill a man to the marrow of his bones. Vince had brought a tantalizing supply of handguns with which to bargain.

"Hi, I'm Vinnie, this is Phil." Vince nodded and reached to shake Rivers' hand.

"Hey, guys. Good to meet you. Where's Lenny?"

"Something came up, and he couldn't make it. But we've got everything covered."

Rivers looked them over with all caution. Moon chose a hit man like some people might shop for a car: he wanted good looks, efficiency, and the most "bang" for the buck, pun intended. Robert "Shooter" (Phil) McCarty was a savvy undercover police officer working out of Port Huron. He was about as handsome as Moon was homely, especially with his shaggy hair and beard. Moon thought Shooter looked like a mafia hit man, and he really was a close replica. His chiseled features, his long, shiny black hair, and his gang-like clothes – he was unmistakably someone who carried a good deal of clout.

Joseph J. "Joe" Vince (Vinnie) was a special agent with the Bureau of Alcohol, Tobacco,

Firearms and Explosives. He would later become head of National Intelligence for ATF, and eventually Chief of the Firearms Enforcement Division for them.

"You want a drink, Rivers?" Vince said. "I'll get us something out of the machine.

"7 up or Coke is good. Coke will probably be alright."

"Give me the key to the room," McCarty said to Vince.

While Vince got the drinks, McCarty took the bucket from beside the sink and filled it with ice, then clunked some change into the vending machine, retrieved a Reece's cup, unwrapped it, and tossed the shiny orange paper in the trash can.

Let me show you a sample of this stuff. See what you think of it," Vince said after they were all safely in the room.

Nona was slowly shaking her head.

"I think these will give us some problems." Rivers said, pulling a tall bottle from a paper bag, and mixing a bit with his Coke.

It was obvious to them that Nona was influencing her husband. "No offence to your wife, but I'm surprised you brought her along," Vince said, glancing apprehensively at Nona. "Sorry, ma'am, but we usually only deal with one person at a time."

"Don't worry, she's cool. Nona knows I'm a crook, and what's more, she knows guns even better than I do," Rivers said.

Vince nodded and rubbed his chin, his head cocked to one side. "Hey, I want to set up somethin' regular with you, so let us know if you're interested. How you work it is your business. But let me tell you, they're good. They won't give you any trouble."

"You don't think so?" Rivers said, his eyes radiating surprise.

"No, no, I haven't had any. And where they're gettin' 'em is cool."

"The serial numbers, are they all right in a row?"

"I think every book has numbers runnin' like these," Vince said.

"Yeah, but each book is different. Do they run in sequence? That's what I'm askin' you."

"Just those," Vince said, trying to stay calm.

"There's 83, 82..."

"Yeah, we can mix them up next time down. There's a good chance everybody makes money on this deal. We'll treat you right on the price. But, hey, I'm cool if you don't want to do it, I understand. Everybody's gotta be happy."

"Well, like I said, my wife's scared of them. She's the expert on the rules on guns. She learned from the best in the business. When they run in sequence, we'll run into trouble."

"I know you're just bein' cautious. You want to mix them up, Rivers?"

"Yeah. That would be better, I would think."

"Well, we can do that. But this time, this is all we brought."

"To run a big bunch of them through my store, I could get by with it," Rivers said reluctantly, glancing at Nona.

"Okay, as long as you're gonna be happy with it, and you know this is somethin' you want to do...hey, I'm not pushin' you."'

"How much?"

"Well, are we gonna be doin' business for a while?"

"I want to."

"With some guys with small orders I go 80%. How about 75% of wholesale? You know, since we'll be doing more business. And if I find some more reasonable, I'll pass the savings on to you next time."

"Did your friend tell you what I want done?" Rivers said, attempting to get to the pressing matter on his mind.

"As far as what goes? What do you mean?" Vince said.

"What I've got to have done. Did he say..." Rivers was beginning to question whether Lenny had even mentioned the hit.

"Are you talkin' about the guns? Right. Okay, first of all, I didn't tell him everything I'm doin'. Now you know that's obvious. You know better."

"I think he's talkin' about the other deal," McCarty spoke for the first time.

"Well I'm talkin' about both right now. Go ahead on this." The lines on Rivers' face relaxed.

"Okay," Vince said, "well I don't want him to know everything we're doin'. Okay, I've worked with him, and he's good. I mean he keeps his mouth shut, and he does what he has to, and the only thing I worry about, you know, at times, he used to drink, but he's off it now, and Lenny's been doin' good, and everything we've ever done has been super. And they are going out of the country. It's my tail end, too, you know."

"That's right," McCarty said.

"Okay, they're doin' two things, they're scratchin' them off, then he makes new numbers and puts them on, but makin' them look nice. Like if it's a 1, he makes it a 7, a 6, he makes an 8, and so forth. This is the new ones, and this is somethin' that I'm really able to get into now 'cause I've got such a good connection. This is somethin' that I never have had before, and I'm excited about it, because it has really worked out great. And there's a good market for this sort of thing. Supply and demand, that's what keeps the wheels turnin'."

"But the price of these? If I figured right, based on wholesale and what you told me, it would put my cost on these at just three grand. Is that right?" Rivers said, mixing another drink. Immediately he wondered if he should have used the word "just".

"Hey, right. You're pretty darn good at figures, aren't you? Where's mine?" Vince said. "Just give me a little of your rum and Coke. That'll seal the deal."

"Well, I figure in my head. I think I can move these babies. And I've got, I know, at least a couple of guys who are trying to round up some hand guns."

"I know I can come up with some Smiths. And also sawed-off shotguns, crap like that. We've had some calls for them."

Chapter Eight

"Nona, didn't you have some shoppin' you needed to do? There's a nice mall out 75 North a ways. What's it called, Hamilton Place?"

"Sure, Clint. I need to find a new coat, and maybe some shoes. Give me the car keys, and I'll be out of your hair. Nice meetin' you guys."

It was the first time that Nona had uttered a word. Vince and Mc Carty were beginning to wonder about her vocal skills. After the door had shut, Rivers felt free to speak his mind.

"Now that we've got our gun business taken care of, and Nona's out, I've got to tell you fellows, I'm in trouble. That's why I need to get that other job taken care of. I got this guy breathin' right down my goldern neck!"

"Okay," Vince said quietly.

"Bad." Rivers was shaking his head.

"Let me tell you on that, now. I hope we're gonna do business. I wantta make you happy," Vince said, "Hey, man, Phil here will take care of that. But we're gonna do it the right way. If we're gonna do this hit, we're gonna look at the guy first, it's not gonna be some quick, 'wham-bam, thank you ma'am' type thing."

"I don't want it that way." Rivers took another sip of his drink, and lit a cigar.

"But we want to give you a break on the price," Vince said, as if reminding McCarty, "so we want you to do a little work for us.

When we look at the guy, we want to know who his girlfriend is, we want to know everything there is to know about this guy. And we want to know what he does. We don't want to do it in front of his family. No problems like that. Or in front of anybody else, for that matter."

"Do you want it to be an accident?" McCarty said.

"I wish he could just vanish." Rivers took a big puff on his cigar, and blew a smoke ring.

"Do you want him to just…"

"I wish he could just vanish," Rivers repeated, breaking in on McCarty.

"Who is he? Is he some kind of a big-wig?" McCarty said.

"Yes, he is."

"What is he?"

"Sheriff."

"Where you live?" Vince said.

"Yep."

"Okay, now, it's gonna be a little more dough for that. You know, 'cause he's a cop," McCarty said in a gruff tone.

"It isn't gonna make any difference there, 'cause they'll think everybody in Moore County done it."

"That's cool. The guy's hated?"

"He's hated somethin' fierce."

"What's he, a rotten cop? Taking money on the side or somethin'?"

"No. I think he's just a nigger lover, for one thing. And he rides everybody. This other guy wanted me to do it, but, that's out. I just can't do somethin' like that."

Vince frowned. "Okay, wait a minute. I don't like dealin' with someone I haven't met. I don't know, Rivers."

"You ain't gonna deal with nobody but me."

Vince raised his hand and twisted his head to the left. "Okay, all right."

"Hey, that's why I was a little late this afternoon. I went by and talked to him, and he said everything was up to me. He doesn't want to know you guys."

"That's cool," Vince said.

"Just me."

"I only want to deal with you," McCarty nodded, pointing at Rivers, and shaking his finger briskly.

"He don't know anything. Only that I was gonna meet a guy over here."

"Okay."

"He don't even know where you're from."

"That's cool. That's why we don't want anybody else involved, you know," Vince said.

"Your wife doesn't know anything about this?" McCarty said, frowning.

"The only thing she knows is that we came over here to look at guns. Now she knows we talked about needin' him out of the way, but she don't know that I'm talkin' to you about this today. I thought it would be better to talk this deal just man to man. I'll fill her in later."

"Hey, we're gonna get all of the details down. We'll tell you when we're gonna do this, but we've gotta pick the time and the place," Vince said.

"Right, yeah, and like I said, I don't think you've got a thing to worry about if you just went right down there and did it. 'Cause not long ago he was shot at four times."

"That helps!" McCarty smiled.

"Yeah, right," Vince agreed.

"It's too bad they missed him."

"Yeah, but we don't like to rush into anything like this. You understand?" McCarty said firmly.

"Yeah."

"Okay, we want to be careful."

"He's being overly cautious, so he may have somebody with him at all times, I don't know."

"Give me one of those cigars, will you?" Vince urged, extending his hand toward Rivers.

"But he's only got two deputies. That's all."

"Hey, Rivers, is he married?" McCarty said,

"Yeah."

"Where's he live? Do you know?"

"The jail."

"At the *jail*?" Mc Carty seemed dumbfounded. He'd never heard of a law official living in the building where he worked.

"But he leaves all the time. He just bugs everybody to death. How he even got reelected, I'll never know. I've gotta put up with him four more years if we don't get rid of him, 'cause he just got elected."

"Can you get a picture of him?"

"Yeah." Rivers' eyes batted and he made a slight frown.

"And we want to know about the rides he has. His cruiser and his personal ride. That's important."

"Right now he only has one car at the department. That's a problem."

"That's the sheriff's car?" Mc Carty stretched and yawned.

"Yeah. There's only one."

"Does he drive it everywhere he goes?"

"Most of the time."

"But what about a personal car?"

"He's got a station wagon, but his wife usually has that. I never see him out in that unless he's off duty. And that's almost never, except Sunday."

"Where's the jail in Lynchburg?"

"Right downtown." Rivers got up and walked around, rubbing his right leg.

"What's the problem, rheumatism or nerves?" Vince asked.

"Neither, my leg's just goin' to sleep," Rivers said with a grunt.

"You know, I just thought of somethin'. How about explosives? You got any?" McCarty said.

"Uh-huh," Rivers nodded.

"That might be the best way," Vince said. "They don't leave any trace of anything. We won't even have to be there when it happens."

"Well, of course... do you want him missin', or do you care?" McCarty said.

"I don't really care. I would rather he just disappear, but I don't really care. I just want him off my tail."

"Does he travel any place? Out of state anywhere?" McCarty said.

"No. Only to pick up somebody. But he's the type who catches everybody. So help me. I don't know how he does it. Nobody can get away with anything in that little hillbilly town!"

"You know that timing device that you have? It would be good. Can you get the caps?" Vince said, turning toward McCarty.

"They're blasting around there every day," Rivers said, "and I've got caps, too, if you need 'em."

"Don't take *anything* out of your store. We need stuff that can't be traced. They'll never put this stuff on us if we do it right."

"The trouble is gettin' into a small town like that and gettin' back out, especially if this guy knows everybody's every move, right?" McCarty said.

"Yeah, that's my point. A Georgia car can drive through town and he's gotta stop them just to see who they are. That's the kind…"

"If we came through town with Michigan plates..." McCarty broke in, only to be crowded out by Rivers.

"You wouldn't want to do that. You want a Tennessee car."

Vince was calm. "That'll be no problem. We've got to get our heads together and plan it to the tee."

"It's like I said. I can get you a picture..."

"Something from when he got elected or..."

"Shoot, man. There were oodles and gobs of them plastered around town. I can probably still get one off a tree." Rivers could feel the pieces beginning to fit in the puzzle. *Was this for real? Could their problems be almost over?*

"How many police did you say they had? Is it just him and his deputies?" McCarty said.

"Got a light?" Vince said, only to be ignored.

Chapter Nine

"Nope. You got one state trooper, and he hates the sheriff," Rivers said. "He sat right down in the store the other night and told me the two of them may end up in a gun fight. Can you believe it? The dang state trooper even hates his guts." Rivers laughed. "Then you've got the city. There's two of them. They've just got one car, though; one for the state and one for the city in Moore County. The two from the city are usually together at night, and only one works in the daytime. The sheriff has only got two real deputies, like I told you. He's got another guy who volunteers; he's not on the payroll, though. They've only got one car. They've got another one that's been wrecked. He can't even get the county to spring to fix it right now." Rivers threw back his head and laughed.

"I like this more and more," Vince said with a nod and a grin.

"One car for his whole department, huh?" McCarty seemed to want to make sure he had been hearing right. *Maybe this is funny*, he thought. "Are all the cops right in town?"

"Yeah, right in town."

"I'd like to get him out of town then."

"Hey, just make a call," Vince said.

"That's all you gotta do." Rivers nodded.

"We'll even try a couple of times and see how it works."

"Let's see, he lives right in town, though?" McCarty asked.

"Yeah, in the building where his office is."

"Is that like a house or an office building?"

"Well, it's what I think used to be an old house. It's really an old jail, is what it is. He's got somebody on the radio there. It's usually this girl my wife knows."

Girl his wife knows? Vince thought. *Could they have an inside contact?*

"You think we should do them all in the building? Or it doesn't matter to you?" McCarty said.

"I think it'll be better to get him out of town in his car," Vince came back, "but you're the expert though."

"I think you're right. Out of town will be better. I just like to have a backup plan."

"We've got a trip we have to make next week. You're not in a big rush, are you, Rivers? I mean like if it takes a couple or three weeks to get this pulled off, would that be okay?"

"Hey, it's like I said, somebody's gotta do it. If we don't get it done, the other guy's gonna do it himself, and I don't want to see him try it."

"Yeah."

"He begged me two weeks ago just to get him over to his house. 'I'll do it,' he said. He's upset over a stolen tractor that the sheriff is looking for. He said, 'tell him I've got the goldarn thing in my basement.' Well, I told the sheriff, alright, but he ain't takin' the chance of goin' over there."

"He knows better, huh?"

"There's a lot of people mad at him," McCarty said, "It's not going to bring any…"

"I don't think anybody would worry about it. Heck, I don't even think the state would miss him. How he got elected, I'll never know. I think the niggers put him in."

"I tell you what, get what you need from him, Phil, and let's get to work on this. Let the man know your price, though, and give him a break, too."

"Well, you get me five grand. That should do it. Okay?"

"That's fine with me. I'll have it when the job's done. You seen Walkin' Tall, didn't you?" Rivers said with a serious look on his face.

"Yeah."

"That's him."

"Another goody two-shoes, huh?"

"Usually I charge a little more with somebody like him, but if we're gonna be doing business... I guess what I really want to be sure of, are you sure the people around there are totally POed with this guy?" McCarty said.

"Oh, yeah! Like I said, nobody likes him. The city hates his guts, now that's what's bad.

When the city and the state and the county can't even sit down at a table together, and they can't even do that."

"What's his name?"

"Cunningham. Ron Cunningham."

"That doesn't sound like a southern name. What's he on your butt about now?"

"Stolen car."

"Does he think it's you just 'cause you live in town, is that it?"

"I know he's already got my record from up north, and I hate that. He's just that type. He'd go right up there and get my record, and I've got a record a mile long."

McCarty clicked his jaw. He knew it was imperative to act worried. His gut told him that if he didn't, Rivers might have concern about his validity. "Do we need to get our guns out of Lynchburg?"

"No, no. That's good. Lenny helps me keep that taken care of," Rivers assured him, lying back on the bed, and scanning the ceiling with his piercing eyes.

"I trust my man, Lenny, implicitly," McCarty said. "He'll take the blame for stuff, and I treat him right. He's the kind of help you need. He knows where his bread is comin' from. Hey, we're tryin' to get out of the state no later than Sunday. Can you get some of this together for us?"

"Your money is good. Don't sweat it." Rivers plunged upward and stared McCarty in the eyes.

"Now we may not be able to get back here for, you know, a few weeks."

"You know what to do if you want me," Rivers said.

"You do live in the same area, right?"

"Yeah. The other guy I told you about lives there, too. This should be kept simple."

"Just remember, we don't want anything that will bring the heat in. That's one thing my dad always said. It's like this Blanton guy. You know, he brings heat on himself. We're just trying to make a buck. We don't need heat. We're just bein' straight up with you."

"In the daytime you'll be fine in Lynchburg. There are busloads of tourists going through Jack Daniel's."

"We'll go through Jack Daniel's and let 'em see us there. We might even pick up a couple of honeys," McCarty said with a wicked chuckle.

"You think we should get a Tennessee car?" Vince said in a raspy tone. "Dang! I've got a freakin' frog in my throat.

"No, I know I said that might be best, but after I thought about it, in the daytime you'd be fine. At nighttime you'd stick out like a sore thumb in an out-of-state car. After 6:00 or 7:00 o'clock you got no business there. That's just the way the sheriff feels. He was standin' out in front of my store one night, and I was talkin' to him, and this Alabama car went by, and he said, 'wasn't that an Alabama license?' I said, 'I don't know, I didn't even look at it, you know,' and he says, 'Come on with me,' and I jumped in the car with him. He stopped the car about a mile down the road and wanted to know what the guy was doin' in Moore County. This was after dark, and he thinks the guy has got no business bein' there."

"You must have him trustin' you pretty much, now. I think you could talk your way out of anything, Rivers." Vince grinned, opening the curtain and glancing out.

"Well, that's just the way I've learned to do with him. I don't argue with his logic."

"Is this other guy a cop or anything? The other guy who wants him knocked off?" McCarty said, reaching for his glass, and shaking around the ice which was now melting, while the muscles in his face tightened.

"No."

"Oh well, that ain't bad, then." McCarty let his face return to normal, and began to paste on a fake smile.

"Let me call you. Lenny's been callin' me too dang much. I don't trust my phone. My line is..."

"Hey, I don't blame you. If there's something fishy on your line," Vince jumped in, seemingly wanting to break the somber mood.

"Call me from a pay phone," McCarty said, "some place out of town. Leave the pay phone number, and let me go somewhere else and get back to you. We can do the same if we need to chat with you."

"Yeah, I've been hearin' somethin' funny on my line…"

"Like a clickin' or somethin'?"

"Yeah." Rivers licked his dry lips, and scratched the back of his head in an up-and-down motion.

"I'll tell you though, Lenny's pretty sharp. He can hear crap like that. Of course you never can tell. You're not a dummy yourself. I like you. You're being careful," Vince said.

"I don't know you guys, either." Rivers seemed a bit edgy.

"Well, yeah, but it works both ways, right?" McCarty said.

They all joined in a nervous laugh.

Chapter Ten

"I tell you right now..." Vince started, but was cut off by Rivers.

"I was a little leery comin' over here, 'cause I don't know you guys, you look awful familiar, I don't know why," he said, gazing at McCarty.

"How the *heck* come do you think I look familiar?" McCarty said. From his tone, Rivers knew he'd better have a darn good reason, but didn't have one on the tip of his tongue.

"I don't know."

"Unless you've ever been to Port Huron," McCarty said, looking Rivers directly in the eye.

"That's the only place I ever knew you from," said Vince, "except when you go with those broads down to Florida," he guffawed. "Did you ever stop in L-l-lynchburg, Tennessee?" Vince drawled, placing his left fist against his side, and looking upward at McCarty, as he playfully tilted his chin downward.

"Unless you've been out to Vegas," McCarty said, ignoring Vince's comical insinuation.

"No, I've never been out there," Rivers said, ever so sincerely, holding his brow.

"Of course everybody tells me I look like a guy who does the news on TV."

"Yeah! Who is that guy? That's, uh... Cronkite?" Vince said with a grin.

"No! This guy's not there anymore. He used to be on in Detroit. But he wore glasses. I don't wear glasses!"

Seated on the bed, Rivers stroked his chin with his thumb and forefinger, closed his eyes, and took a deep breath.

"I don't want to give you the thumbs up on this," McCarty started again, "if you have any doubts about me. We've just all got to be comfortable with each other, and with doin' this. If I'm gonna stick my neck out, I don't want you gettin' cold feet."

Rivers raised his head and looked straight at McCarty. "No, like I said. I'm good to go."

"And the money's a sure thing? What if this other fellow says, 'I don't know this guy, and I don't know if I'm payin' him anything?'"

"It won't be like that. He's got it in the bank, and when we know the time has come, and it's being done, I can draw it out. He's left it all up to me. He trusts me, and I trust him. He knows if I don't pay, it will mean I'm taken out, too. This guy won't let me get killed."

"If you want to stand good for the five g's, okay," McCarty said sternly.

"I'll stand good for it, 'cause I know that if I had asked him, he'd have given it to me before I came over here today. But I'm not givin' it to you till the deed is done."

"After we do a deal, and I move on up the road, I can't hack goin' to jail."

"Me either," Rivers agreed.

"Oh, heck, no," Vince said.

"I've done been there one time, and I don't want to go back," Rivers said.

"Hard time?" McCarty said.

"No, no, just in the county, ninety days." It was just easier not telling the whole truth by admitting his stint in the Michigan prison.

"Oh, shoot! That ain't nothin'!" McCarty said with a chuckle.

"I only served four of it." Rivers cocked his head back and grinned.

"Four days?"

"Felt like ninety."

"How'd you pull that off? Blanton was the sheriff then, or somethin'?" Vince said jokingly.

"No, man. That was in Florida. Paid off the judge, same thing."

"Hey, I like this guy more all the time," Vince said.

"Cost me a house."

"What? For a ninety day rap it cost you that much? Jiminy Cricket!" Vince seemed floored.

"Did you stand good for the bucks then?" McCarty said.

"You'll get your money!" Rivers said emphatically, a frown in his brow.

"Hey, like I said. Once I'm on the road, everything's cool. There ain't nobody gonna give us guns and let us truck with them," McCarty reminded him.

"How long is it gonna take for you to get us what we need?" Vince said.

"I'll get you a poster off a tree or somethin'. That will be simple. I had a whole bushel basket full of 'em at the store, but I don't know what happened to them."

"See, he's a fan of the man!" Vince joked.

"Once you see a picture of him, you can't miss this sucker."

"You know cops. They all look alike in uniform," McCarty said as if he really meant it.

"He don't wear a uniform most of the time."

"I tell you, I can smell a cop a mile away," McCarty said with a scowl.

"He just wears sports clothes most of the time. Walkin' Tall. He's that type."

"Yeah, hot dog! He got a stick, too?"

"I've never seen it, but I hear he has used one. Like I told you guys, he's Johnny-on-the-spot all the time. I called him at 6:00 one morning, and told him that there was a cow in front of my store, come and get it, and he did. He jumped out of bed and drove right down to the store. I just had to see if he would come out.

Everybody in Lynchburg is gonna be a suspect, me included."

"That's cool!" Vince said, leaning back in his chair.

"This guy who wants it done, now he's going to be the worst suspect of all. But he'd do it himself before much longer."

"My daddy always said, 'if you can't play the game, don't get in the middle of it," Vince said with a smirk."

"I know he don't want a cheap botched job," Rivers said.

"It will be done right," McCarty said, nodding.

"Right. That's what he wants." Rivers' face was straight and his eyes had a weighty stare.

"I can vouch for him," said Vince.

"I know I could go over to Huntsville and get it done for $500, but it wouldn't be done right."

"That would just get you in a jam," McCarty said, with a slight raise of his left eyebrow, his left hand resting on his chin.

"I think we've got a good thing goin' on the pieces. We can do a lot more business after this mess is history. There's always a good market for guns of all kinds." Rivers seemed calmer.

"We'll get back to our suppliers tomorrow and see how many of which piece we can get at the same time." Vince knew that they had reached a point of confidence.

"I'll get back to you soon," Rivers said.

The day had worn rapidly on, and early winter darkness was beginning to fall as a heavy blanket.

"What time is it getting' to be? We might want to get out of here and party or somethin'." Vince said. "I hate to set around a stinkin' motel room all night."

"What time would you be goin' out?" Rivers said.

"Well, we want to leave no later than maybe 7:00 o'clock ...."

"Hey, you want another cigar?" Rivers asked.

"No," Vince said. "Hey Phil, you're drivin', man. We can go whenever you get good and ready. It's up to you. I don't care."

"Hey, man, can you call us tomorrow? You and Nona might as well spend the night here, since she's still out shopping. She'll be tired when she gets back," McCarty said.

"Can you call us about 2:00 or 3:00?" Vince said.

"Does that give you time enough to talk about this stuff with your wife? And let that other guy know what's goin' on?" McCarty said.

"Well, I'll get out of here first thing in the morning, and go over and talk with that guy. I better make it about 4:00."

"That's our time or yours?" McCarty said.

"That's your time."

"Okay. Four our time. I'll keep our rooms and I'll be here till you call. I want to get the heck out of here as soon as possible."

"We just need to get all the merchandise gone from here as soon as possible."

"We'll both stick around."

Chapter Eleven

"Hey, we still didn't talk about the stamps. What do you want to do on them? How much you want?" Vince said.

"My wife is worried to death about that," Rivers said, taking in a large gulp of air. "That's why I didn't mention them. One thing I talked to her about...."

"I tell you what, would you like to take one and show her, and then decide tomorrow? They're good. It's the way we're doin' it."

"What the heck are you doin'? Just tell me, were they stolen?" Rivers sneered as he talked.

"No," Vince said.

"They're not stolen?" Rivers said in unbelief.

"They're not stolen," Vince said.

"They're not *reported* stolen!" Rivers mocked.

"They're not reported stolen," Vince repeated, "Okay, what I'm trying to say is that I've got an aunt and uncle in the food stamp business, right? Okay?"

"Well, that way it's probably okay," Rivers said.

"Right. That's what I'm trying to tell you, see, some guys worry that they are counterfeit, and they're not. They're good stuff. Wait till you see their quality."

"I was lookin' at some before I came over here. Some other stamps. I know what to look for. I like this guy! He's dang careful. Gosh," Vince said.

"Yeah, he's got his ducks in a row," McCarty said with a grin. "Well, would you like to take one for your wife to see?"

"Yeah. I'd like to. But what do I have to do to convince her? She don't want no static. She don't want Daddy goin' to jail."

"Hey, I don't blame her there," Vince said.

"Yeah, 'cause it already cost her a house to get him out!" McCarty echoed.

"Right. Well, you know your wife better than I do! Are you sure she's cool with the stuff we're doin', cause we all lose if something goes wrong."

"Like I told you, Nona knows I'm crookeder than the devil."

"Alright."

"She knows that I wouldn't even be here if both guys both weren't just as much of a..." Rivers allowed a chuckle to stop his sentence, "crook!" he finished.

"You know, I'm surprised that you're traveling with your old lady. I'd have suspected you to bring some broad along, or somethin', you know, to spend the night with you." Vince said.

Rivers tensed. "She goes everywhere with me. I was married once before, and this one's different. She knows most of my business."

"Yeah."

"You might want to keep some things to yourself," McCarty said.

"Yeah," Vince repeated.

"The food stamps, then, maybe you'd like to keep that to yourself if there may be some flack."

"I'll take one and talk to her in the morning. I just can't get my mind off of the problems I've been havin' with the dang sheriff. I'll be glad when that deal is done. I've been down here less than a year and he's been on me like a duck on a June bug."

"Hey, leave that to Phil," Vince said.

"And up in Flint, with all the police they have up there, they never bothered you?"

"They just don't have a Ron Cunningham."

"Gees. I guess not."

"Well, we'll talk to you about these stamps when we call tomorrow. We'll probably be out late, so we're out of here. We'll treat you right on the price. They're good. Here. What do you think?"

"Yeah. They look good."

"Gee, I hope she'll go along with it. I knew you'd like what you saw."

"Well, she'll have to approve everything. The store's even hers."

"You'll have a busy day tomorrow."

"I'm putting this cash in my jacket pocket, and we'll talk tomorrow," McCarty said.

"Yeah, you've made it a busy day for me."

"And we'll have these stamps when we get back together," McCarty said.

"See you," Vince said, as the two left, and McCarty closed the door.

Chapter Twelve

Unaware of the plot brewing to free him from the bonds of his earthly body, Ron was having to deal with another bizarre murder.

At 5:01 AM he was awakened by the unwelcome ringing of his phone.

"Sheriff, when the slop truck came to my barn this mornin', he went to get the old black fellow to help him that I was lettin' stay in my shed. He found him there settin' in a chair, deader'n a nit." The tone of the man's voice was so genuine that Ron knew that it was no prank. He was familiar with the caller, a well-known farmer around Moore County.

"Thanks for calling me, Bill. I'll get hold of the ambulance and the coroner and be right on out. What's the dead man's name?"

"Tanner, Tanner Jackson."

The fog was hanging in the dips as if it had been poured from heaven as Ron drove to the farm. The temperatures were equally low.

"Don't move that body. I've got to get a close look at what happened here," Ron said to the paramedic.

"There's a couple of beer bottles over here. Looks like the old gent had just been drinking and fell and hit his head on that pot-bellied stove." The coroner was leaning over the slumped body.

"Well, I'm going to do some investigating here. Let's not jump to any conclusions. Here's a stick that looks like it may have been used to hit him. Blood's coming out of his mouth and nose, as well as the gash on his head. That doesn't look like a cut and dried case to me. I'm ordering an autopsy."

◆ ◆ ◆

"Joe Grogan, I'm Ron Cunningham, the sheriff over in Moore County. I noticed that the bottles we picked up at the shed where old Tanner Jackson's body was found is the brand you sell here in Tullahoma at your bar. Tanner's autopsy results showed that he had been hit in the head with a blunt object. My bet is the stick of firewood I found near his chair. Did you happen to see him in here that night?"

"Yes, Sheriff. I know who you are. I live in Moore County. Dang shame it's dry. Tanner was in here with a guy named Bob Larkin. They were drinking quite a bit. But the paper said that the coroner had ruled the death accidental, so I didn't give it any thought."

"Well, that's what he assumed. So I decided to keep my feelings quiet until I could get the autopsy results. Did you hear any fuss between these guys that night?"

"Naw. No more than regular cuttin' up. They were always carrying on with one another."

"Where do you think I could find this Bob guy this time of day?"

"He hangs out at the White Rabbit in the middle of the day. You've probably seen him there. I know you eat there sometimes. He's a tall drink of water. And slim."

"Tall slender fella, huh?"

"Yeah. I'd say about your height. And dark complexioned."

"I've seen a guy like that around there. Thanks. I'll find him."

♦ ♦ ♦

"Hey, are you Bob Larkin?"

"Yeah, that's me. What can I do you for, sheriff? Have a seat." Bob took a puff off his Viceroy and blew smoke out of the corner of his mouth.

Ron pulled out a stool and joined Bob at the counter.

"Joe Grogan tells me that you were in the Monkey's Uncle Saloon the night that Tanner Jackson was killed."

"Killed? The paper said…"

"That was before the autopsy results came in. Tanner was hit in the head with a blunt object. And there were some small splinters in his skin. Something like a stick of firewood, wouldn't you think?"

"I don't know what you're talkin' about, Sheriff. I was with him at the bar, but I let him out of my car at the Smith farm. He was very much alive when I last saw him."

"You were driving?"

"Uh, no... we'd had a bit to drink. We were with another guy."

"Who? Who were you with?"

"How should I know? Some guy gave us a lift when we left the bar."

"Then how come you said you let him out?"

"We were in the back seat and I opened the door for him."

"Where did you go?"

"He took me home."

"Can anyone vouch for that?"

"Sure. My mother. I live on Bobo Holler Road. Check it out."

"What time did you get there?"

"About midnight."

"Don't leave town. I may have some more questions."

♦ ♦ ♦

The door slowly opened, and a tiny head peeped into the cold January air.

"Hello?"

"Mrs. Larkin, I'm Sheriff Cunningham. I need to ask you a few questions about your son."

"My God! What has he done now?"

"Ma'am, we don't know that he did anything. This is just a routine investigation."

"Well, come on in. Ain't no need to stand out in the cold."

"Mrs. Larkin, your son was the last person known to see Tanner Jackson alive."

"You mean the old black man who was found out at the Smith farm a couple of weeks ago?"

"Yes, ma'am. He says he got in about midnight that night from Tullahoma. Do you remember?"

"Lands, no. I'm sorry, but I gotta be truthful. I don't wait up for the boy any more. He's a growed man, and I stopped playing nursemaid a long time ago. He's just like everybody else, he's gotta answer to God one day, you know. Now th' boy aint no killer. I just don't think he could do nothin' like that, but I cain't say what time he come home any partic'lar night."

"Thank you, ma'am. I appreciate your honesty. Have a good day."

◆ ◆ ◆

"Bob, I asked you to come in today because there are no other witnesses of what happened that night. I'm afraid your mother couldn't validate your story. No one has come forward saying that they took you home, either. I need you to take a polygraph test."

"A what?"

"Polygraph. A lie detector test. I'm going to ask you this set of questions without the polygraph, then the same questions with the polygraph."

"Uh… Okay, I guess."

"Is your name Robert Lawson?"

"Yes."

"Do you live with your mother on Bobo Hollow Road?"

"Yes."

"Have you ever been to the Monkey's Uncle Saloon in Tullahoma?"

"Yeah, sure."

"Did you personally know a man named Tanner Jackson, now deceased?"

"Yeah, of course."

"Were you with Tanner Jackson on the night of January 5th at the Monkey's Uncle Saloon in Tullahoma?"

"Yes."

"Did you leave the bar with Tanner Jackson that night?"

"Yes. I said that before."

"Did you go into the shed in front of the big barn at the Smith farm with him that night?"

"No! I told you I didn't, by cracky!"

"Just answer the questions, 'yes', or 'no', please. Did you have an argument with Tanner that night?"

"No!"

"Did you take a stick of wood and hit Tanner in the head with it?"

"No, dern it! No, heck no."

"Calm down, Bob. If you are having trouble now, it's going to be worse with the polygraph. You look a little nervous. Did any of those questions bother you?"

Bob squirmed and took in a large gulp of air.

"Yes."

"Which questions bothered you?"

"The ones about what happened in the shed."

"Are you ready to tell me what really happened?"

"You're gonna get me with that machine anyway. Yeah, I hit him! We had an argument over a girl. I used to date her, and he said he had slept with her. It made me furious. I didn't mean to kill him. But I couldn't take it. I still have feelings for her."

"Robert Larkin, you're under arrest for the murder of Tanner Jackson. Anything you say can and will be used against you in a court of law. You are entitled to an attorney. If you can't afford one, you will be appointed for you by the court. Book him, George."

Bob Larkin was later found guilty of first degree murder.

Chapter Thirteen

Ron was still reeling from the Jackson case. He was understandably a tad on the nervous side when an agent with the Tennessee Bureau of Investigation called and invited him to meet him and an agent with the FBI at Shoney's Restaurant in Tullahoma. He was even shakier when he was informed that this odd collection of gentlemen had been hired to take him out. Nonetheless, he would certainly follow their orders explicitly.

"Do you know anyone who wants you dead?" the FBI agent said.

Ron's mind sought after valid reasons that someone might want him killed, but it didn't take long to find suspects. The situation with James was first to come to mind, and for very good reasons; ones which he would keep to himself until he was more certain about the present circumstances. But he had much earlier experienced some hairy ordeals. The problems had started while he was still a deputy under Chuck Johnson.

♦ ♦ ♦

" ♫ Shall we gather at the river, the beautiful, the beautiful river, gather with the saints at the river that flows by the throne of God... ♪"

"Ron, there's a local deputy out here wanting you to come with him. He says it's urgent," an usher whispered.

"I hope it is, getting us out of church like this. Come on Linda, get the kids."

"Ron," the sheriff said, "there's a big problem out here at Redd's Grocery. Get out here, pronto! There's a motorcycle gang in the area jerking women out of cars and raping them. God knows what else you'll run into."

"Have Larry bring my cruiser out there. See you in a bit."

Ron hung up the phone and emitted a deep sigh. It was Sunday night. He'd been escorted from the church in Winchester to the Franklin County Sheriff's Department.

"You gonna need some help?" The local sheriff asked.

"I expect I will. I appreciate all the help I can get."

Their blue lights flashing their rhythmic message, and the night air crashing about them, two Franklin County patrol cars followed Ron to Chestnut Ridge Road in Moore County, not far from where he was living. As they pulled into the gravel lot in front of the store, the scene awaiting them was total bedlam. The lot was packed. Anxious neighbors had noisily congregated with the sheriff, his son, Larry and the store owner and his wife. A young girl, her clothes torn and arms scratched and bleeding from the blackberry briars through which she had dashed in her desperate escape, was whimpering and jabbering.

"Ron, it's about time you got here!" the sheriff yelled over the roar of the crowd.

"Somebody's gotta get down there and get those hoodlums. They got gas and drinks and stuff and went off without paying," the distraught storekeeper was trying to be heard.

"Hey, hey! Everybody quiet down! I can't hear myself think! Dang! Linda, you and the kids go on home, I'm taking my cruiser down to the lake and get the low-down on this bunch."

"Are you gonna be alright, Daddy?' Shannon said with a whine.

"Sure, honey. Don't worry about me, you just go on home with Mommy. Daddy will be fine."

Ron eased along the paved street, and onto Shasteen Hollow Road, the gravel lane onto which the sect of Hell's Angels had disappeared. At Tim's Ford Lake, the sight was not a pleasant one. Tattered tents lined the TVA property, and drug-indulged couples lay shamelessly in the grass engaging in sex acts. In the meantime, the gang members had blocked the road with their cycles. Ron pushed hard on the accelerator, plunging his cruiser through the blockade. Mangled motorcycles went flying through the cool night air, tearing up the sod.

Going back to the store, he asked the other deputies to follow him. As they arrived at the brink of a hill on their right, the officers could detect the perpetrators below, and came to a slow stop. A mobile home seemed to be at the center of the problem. Several men were leaning back on their bikes, casually smoking marijuana. The deputies bravely emerged.

"What do we need to do, Ron?"

"Now, boys, let's use our heads for something besides hat racks. There are only three of us, and at least a dozen or more of these loonies. You guys get your shotguns, and be ready to use them if necessary."

"We only have two shotguns in our cars."

"Use mine."

"But what are you gonna do?"

A few weeks earlier Ron had confiscated an aluminum baseball bat from some young ruffians which was being used for something other that its intended purpose. Since he didn't carry a gun, in true Andy Taylor fashion, he now must show his Pusser side with his dogged determination not to be overpowered.

"I got something, don't worry about me."

"What do we do now?" another one said.

"Rack your guns, get ready for action. I'm going in swinging and I'll ask questions later."

The other deputies looked at one another and shrugged, a bit of a sheepish grin on their faces, then eased forward.

As the unmistakable sound of the shotguns cocking penetrated the air, the men on the bikes made a flashing dash behind the unkempt trailer.

"Okay, the first one who opens his mouth, I'll bust his head," Ron yelled, as he marched onward. Suddenly a young boy appeared in the dim light. To Ron's dismay, he was the nephew of a prominent local official.

"Hey Ron, what's goin' on?"

"What the heck are you doing here, Ricky?"

"Just hangin' out. The wrong place at the wrong time, I guess."

Ignoring the boy for the moment, Ron continued his advance, but the next deputy caught Ricky on his jaw with the butt of his gun, rendering him defenseless, and loaded him in his car as blood spurted over the window.

A violently angry gang member plunged toward Ron. Removing the bat from his shoulder, he laid it in the sweaty palm of his left hand, placing his right hand on the bottom end. Sliding it forward, the big end caught the cyclist in the mouth, forcing him down.

Mayhem ensued, as the fiery deputy plowed onward into the face of his foe. Swinging left and right, the gang members continued to drop.

"Who's in charge here? Just who the heck is in charge here?" Ron screamed as he marched.

At once, as if from nowhere, a lady about five feet eight inches tall, and about the same in girth, stormed toward him.

"You stinkin' pig! You get your dern butt out of here, or you're gonna get it whipped but good!"

As he pushed her backward with the end of the bloody bat, her feet caught on the jagged root of a maple, and her huge frame met the ground with a resounding thud. As she moaned and cursed, her husband came toward

Ron, swinging crutches at him. Ron's bat caught first one crutch, then the other, breaking them into splintered pieces, as the enraged man lost his fragile balance and joined his wife in a limp pile on the hard dirt below.

The air reeked heavily with the stench of burning marijuana. The toilet in the mobile home continued to flush with regularity. As Ron glanced downward, he noticed that the trailer had no underpinning and the PVC drain pipe was easily visible. Using the bat again, he crushed the pipe, which released a constant flow of flushed dope.

At that, a giant-of-a-man, whom Ron could have sworn he had seen in James Bond flicks, stormed out the trailer door, ducking to do so.

"I'm in charge here!" he screamed, pausing on the metal step. "Now what the Sam Hill are you gonna do about it?"

Ron wasted not a precious second, as he wielded the heavy bat with both hands, plunging it into his left shoulder with all of the force in his sturdy body. To his amazement, there was no reaction. The man was just angrier, as he came forward with a visage filled with demonic resolve. Ron swung again at the same target. This time the wild man only slightly flinched.

He's going to kill me! Ron's thought was sudden and finalistic. *The next aim is my last shot at this!*

With all diligence, he swung the hefty bat squarely into both knees of his raging opponent, finally forcing him to the ground.

167

The big ogre lay moaning, and screaming, "You broke my legs!" Ron instructed a bystander of the group who had made no effort to fight him to load the battered giant into a nearby truck and drive him to the nearest hospital. Ron then marched from tent-to-tent knocking them flat. The patrol cars were packed and the offenders taken to jail. The nightmare had ended. Or had it? Could some of these men have had a hand in wanting to see him dead?

♦ ♦ ♦

But that was not the only time he had wielded a bat for defense.

One evening that same summer, Ron was home eating supper when the sheriff called. He told Ron that there had been a fight at Barker's Grocery at Parkertown, and asked him to go check it out. He told him who the boy was, and to be careful, "'cause he has a knife and is threatening to cut you to pieces if you came out to get him." When Ron got there, the young man was drunk, and had his hand buried in his pocket. There was only one other person in the store, but he couldn't get out, because the boy, Robby, was between him and the door. Of course, Ron wasn't packing a gun, so he picked up a baseball bat which was lying by the counter, Robby was grinning like a possum, swearing that he was going to cut Ron to shreds. "You might," Ron said, "but you're going to jail, and first you'll be hauled to the hospital. Now lay that knife on the counter, and get in my car before you go out lying down." He did precisely that. But Ron had to fight him to get him into the cell.

And as for James, he had even more reason to suspect him which he would not reveal until this surreal saga played out.

Chapter Fourteen

"I have an idea who might be involved in this," Ron told the agents. "But I can't be sure. I've already been shot at, more than once, and somebody tried to burn the jail down last summer."

As Ron's mind whirred, he relived that horrendous night when he had been led into a planned ambush at a nearby roadside park. That incident had been even more alarming than the attempted burning of the jail. Truly, he had made an undetermined number of enemies. That evening he had been phoned several times, and told that there was a fight in progress at a roadside park, and that someone had been injured. When he got there he saw

171

not a soul. A brilliant flash lit up the darkness, as a shot rang out. One of his side mirrors had been hit. Aiming his shotgun in the direction from which he thought the bullet had come, he began to return fire. As he stealthily eased forward, another shot cried out. It was from the opposite side of the park! He now found himself dodging a stream of angry ammo. Finally, after circling the park, and emptying his shotgun, he was able to return to his cruiser and safely escape the scene.

Another late summer afternoon Ron had been standing between the jail and the hardware store. *What the..?* he thought. It sounded as if a bee had flown past his head. As he swatted at his ear, hoping to deter the critter, he heard a pinging sound, as if rocks were being thrown at the power lines crossing the narrow alley way, but no one was visible.

A slop truck on its way to the distillery to pick up mash for cattle feed came flying toward the square, screeching to a sudden halt directly in front of the jail. Waylon Harriman jumped out and yelled at Ron, "Get out of the street! Somebody up on Tanyard Hill is shooting down toward the square." Suddenly, a shot flew into the gravel next to the sheriff's right leg, ricocheting onto the nearby utility pole. Waylon frantically dove for the open door of his truck. His body animatedly catapulted through the air by the sheer force of determination. Simultaneously, Ron dashed around the corner of the jail. Both were narrowly missed by the wildly flying bullets.

Ron knew that he must find the source. He jumped into his cruiser like an angry crusader and rushed to the only place from which the shots could be originating. There was Clinton Rivers' son-in-law, Jerry Dean Wade, at the stock gap, trying to escape in a battered car. Blocking him in, Ron dragged Wade out and tossed him forcefully into the back of his patrol car. Immediately returning to Wade's car, Ron found three high-powered rifles, both equipped with effective scopes. After retrieving the guns, and making a quick radio call to have the car impounded, Wade was taken directly to jail. During in-depth questioning, he admitted that he had been paid to kill the sheriff by someone who would remain anonymous. But no evidence could conclusively link the solicitation at that time to Rivers.

And, among other incidents, there had been the experience as a deputy when he had flushed an intruder from the County Building and been the target of fire. Linda, who had been working part-time as a dispatcher, had noticed a suspicious person lurking in the area as she was attempting to leave, and radioed Ron. After driving his car to the rear of the building, he saw the intruder run down the hallway toward the back stairs, and focused a spotlight on the rear exterior door. Just as he had emerged from his vehicle, a shrill shot rang forth. Ducking behind his open car door, he glanced up just in time to see a heavy-built figure flit around the building.

While Ron was giving pursuit on foot, the intruder had vanished into the darkness.

A local farmer named Blackburn had then taken pity on him after the Tanyard Hill incident. "I guess you think you're in Mayberry, or something. What's this about not carrying a hand gun?" he had said.

"I've managed to get along pretty well without one."

175

"Here's a .357 Magnum, it may come in handy some day."

"What do you want me to do?" Ron asked the officers who had brought him the news.

"A guy called Phil McCarty will be in touch. He'll have your instructions. We can't let anybody suspect we're onto them."

Chapter Fifteen

On Wednesday, January 25th, Clinton Rivers called the number that he had been given from a pay phone in Tullahoma, and asked for Phil to call him back.

"Hey, man. I got this mug shot of you-know-who. What do I do with it?"

"Just drop it in the mail to P.O. Box 2490 Port Huron, Michigan. I'll take it from there."

"Hold on. I have to write that down, Post Office Box what?"

"2490. That's in Port Huron. Got it?"

"Yeah, got it,"

"I have my plans all set. I'm going down on February 13th. I'm gonna spend some time cruisin' around town. Then I'm gonna make a call to your buddy to meet me out in the country, and I'm gonna take care of him once and for all."

"Sounds like you've thought it through."

"You got that thing right. You and your wife can meet me at that motel where we went before. That is, if your old lady's in the know on this by now."

"Oh, yeah, she knows about it. We've talked. She's cool."

"I'll have you a room reserved. Just tell the desk clerk who you are, and they'll give you your key. Some time that night I'll breeze in and meet with you."

"Yeah, and I've been doing some thinkin', too. I gotta have real proof that you've nailed him. Some old farmer gave him a .357 Magnum, and he carries it on him now. I guess he don't think he's Andy Taylor any more since he's been shot at a couple of times. I want his .357 and his wallet with his ID and badge. But I want one more thing."

"What's that, Rivers?"

I want one of his ears. They're unmistakable. I want his ear. That way I'll know he's really dead."

"I hear you. I'll do my best."

"That's my terms. You bring me those things, and you'll get your money. I'll tell the guy, and he'll let me get it out of the bank, or get it for me, whatever."

"I don't know what time I'll be in, it may be late. Just depends."

"I'm counting on you, man."

"I won't let you down."

"We'll have some pieces with us. We're dealing some, and my wife will be with me, just like last time.

"Sounds good. Remember to tell the desk clerk your name and that you have a reservation. That's all you need to do."

"Don't worry. I heard you loud and clear the first time."

"See you at Chattanooga."

"Bye."

"Later."

Chapter Sixteen

"Sheriff, this is Robert McCarty, code name, 'Shooter'. Rivers knows me as 'Phil'. Meet me at twenty-one hundred hours local time. Where would be a safe place to park your patrol car?"

"Behind Moore County High School, I think, would be best. It's off the beaten path, and after school there's no one around."

"10-4. Now don't you breathe a word of our plan to anyone. Not your deputies, not your best friend, shoot, not even your wife. Got it? Not a soul can know or we're over with this."

◆ ◆ ◆

"Ron Cunningham, it's good to meet you, McCarty." Ron extended his hand and was met by a sturdy grasp.

"The pleasure's all mine. I just wish it weren't under these circumstances. Are you nervous?"

"I'd be a dang liar if I told you I wasn't," Ron said with a twitch of his lip.

"By the way, Ron, good to see you again," Inspector Huckabee said, reaching out his hand.

"Yeah, man. Good to see you, too."

"You got the gun?" Huckabee asked as they drove down the long driveway to highway 55.

"Yeah, this is the gun I'm supposed to kill him with." Shooter looked Ron straight in the eyes without batting his. "Give me your .357 and your wallet with your ID and badge."

Ron was getting antsier by the minute.

"And we need one of your ears. The proof that you are dead will be those three items. We're being paid $5,000 for the hit."

By this time, Ron was ready to make a daring jump from the moving car. He had hidden another handgun in his jacket in case something was amiss.

"Listen, Cunningham, this clown is not someone to be monkied with. One false move and somebody could *really* end up dead. This sting has to go down *perfecto*."

"You're sure as heck not getting either one of my ears!"

Shooter allowed a slight smile to run across his pale, dry lips. "I think I've got that one figured out."

For some time after the initial dialogue of introductions and pleasantries, things were silent. But Ron's brain was working overtime.

As they cruised across the frozen heights of Monteagle Mountain, Shooter cranked down his window and fired his pistol twice. The piercing shots echoed wildly through the cold night air. A distant owl hooted his startled reaction. Ron flinched as he thought of where those bullets were supposed to have ended up.

I could have been dead already, more than once! Ron thoughts again trailed through the ominous past.

Click! The sound of the pin against the shell of the 12 gauge shotgun was reverberating through Ron's subconscious memory.

He had been summoned to a home in which a young drug addict had terrorized members of his own family, who met him in the yard, wringing their hands in fear and frustration. Entering from the rear, Ron eased down the narrow hallway and was venturing left into the small living area in the front of the house where the stupefied man sat on a couch facing him. The shotgun in his hands was staring Ron squarely in the face.

At first view of Ron, he pulled the trigger. Had the shell not been old, damp, and moldy, Ron would likely have been killed.

As this distinct memory faded, Ron recalled with equal wonder another narrow escape. Not carrying a handgun, he had bluffed his way through a hostage situation using his fingers as an assumed weapon.

It had been a steaming summer Sunday when he was called to a simple country chapel. As he pulled over into the church's parking area, a car sped out beside him. A crazed man sat in the back seat holding a shotgun to the head of the terrified driver.

"There he goes! There he goes!" came the cries. The chase lasted only a short distance down the narrow gravel road before the car slid violently into the ditch. Pulling to the opposite side, Ron rolled into the drainage trench, his head and hands sticking up. Pointing his two fingers toward the perpetrator, Ron called out in his authoritative voice, "Alright. Throw out the gun! Now, get out of the car slowly. That's good. Now, face the car, and put your hands behind your head!

As he recalled these close encounters with death, Ron shook his head. Yes, even when no conspiracy existed, he had been miraculously spared at times.

The stunning full moon hung over Monteagle Mountain like a sentinel in the starry heavens, The face upon it appeared so brilliant that it seemed it could speak.

Chapter Seventeen

As they glided into the parking lot of the Sheraton Inn at East Ridge, Ron let out a muffled sigh.

"The whole motel's being staffed by our people," Shooter explained in a tone of candor.

"The cows are out." A waiter said, as they entered. Ron scratched his head. The mood was just too somber and surreal.

"The cows have been gathered and all taken care of," said another voice.

They checked in, and the undercover bellhop escorted them quietly to their room in the rear of the motel.

Three consecutive rooms had been reserved. Rivers and Nona were in the center room. McCarty, dressed in a convincing black leather jacket, hurried Ron into the pre-designated agent quarters. Closed circuit TV allowed Cunningham and the other officers to have complete access to the activities in the Rivers's room. Rivers and Nona sat on the gun-covered bed, casually munching on hamburgers which they had brought in from the nearby McDonalds.

A pecking knock took Rivers to the door. There stood Shooter, leaning in a nonchalant, macho manner against the cold, dark door frame. McCarty could hear the volume on the television slowly fade. Softly, Rivers motioned in his visitor and eased the door to. "Hey, come on in, Phil. Is it over?"

"Yeah, man. I got him, alright. Here's his .357 Magnum, and this is his wallet with all of his ID, and his badge." McCarty smiled and handed them to him.

"Man, the bullet would look good on a belt buckle," Rivers said, pointing the gun at McCarty's fancy belt.

"Ronald R. Cunningham! Son of a gun! That's it, by Jove! Where's his ear? That was the deal, you know. I've got to have one of his ears!"

Shooter sighed. "I'm sorry about that one. I shot him behind the high school on a little bridge. It's kind of funny, as I was startin' to cut off his ear, I saw the headlights of a car comin', and I had to throw his body in the river. I didn't have a choice. I had to get the heck out of Dodge." Shooter flinched when he thought about the possible reaction. He knew that he was taking a chance, because Rivers should have realized that there was no river there.

Nona Rivers put her hands on her face and shrieked. "My God! You really did it! I can't believe it! I'm glad it's over."

"I need my bucks, man, I need my bucks! I've gotta be long gone before they realize Cunningham's dead!" McCarty said impatiently.

"Hey! His stinkin' wallet's still got money in it!" Nona screamed, breaking out in nervous giggles.

"Yeah, yeah! A deal's a deal. Here it is, five big ones, all in C notes. Do you want me to count it?"

"Na. It's been a pleasure doing business with you."

Wham! The door crashed in like an exploding stick of dynamite. "Freeze! FBI! Clinton Rivers, Nona Rivers, you're under arrest for conspiracy to commit murder, and solicitation to take a human life in the case of Sheriff Ron Cunningham, and unlawful possession of firearms. Anything you say can and will be used against you in a court of law. You are entitled to an attorney. If you can't afford one, you will be appointed one by the court."

"You son of a b....." Rivers was numb. His eyes seemed to become as large as saucers.

"Shut up! I've heard enough from your mouth, Rivers!" Cunningham said. "You've got the devil to pay now."

Rivers curled up the left side of his mouth and reached out his hand. "No hard feelings, right?"

Ron instinctively buckled up his fist, and darted toward his would-be killer.

"No! Come on, now," McCarty said, pushing him back. "I understand how you feel. But that would just make matters worse."

Ron took a deep breath, then coolly turned and walked away.

Chapter Eighteen

"Hey! There's his car! This is where he said he was calling from when he was checking on that parked car!"

"Dang! Something's for sure gone down here."

The deputy shined his heavy flashlight into the cold, empty car, and flashed the beam over the dark seat. "Oh, God, no! This looks like blood! Somebody's done him in, for dang sure."

"We've got to get all of the help we can get."

"Roger that. What about the new governor?"

"I don't know anything about Alexander. Let's give him a call."

"Governor Alexander's residence, may I help you?"

"Yes, Mrs. Alexander, please. I hate to call at this late hour. This is Deputy George with the Moore County Sheriff's Office. I have to speak with the governor. It's very urgent."

"Lamar, wake up, it's a deputy from over in Lynchburg. He says it's urgent."

"I'll take it, Honey," the governor yawned and rubbed his eyes as he reached for the receiver.

"Mr. Alexander, we have reason to believe that Sheriff Cunningham may have been the victim of a hit man," George said shakily. "It had come to light that there was a plot to have him

196

killed, and we have been investigating it for the past two weeks. We located his abandoned patrol car tonight after he didn't return to the jail. There is a reddish spot on the seat which appears to be blood."

"I had been notified of the alleged plot, go on."

"We need you to contact the THP and have them put out an APB. We're just a small county with two deputies, as I'm sure you know."

"I'm sorry to hear about this, That's fine with me. And you need to notify the surrounding County Sheriff Departments. Tell them I said to join you in setting up roadblocks around the area. We'll do whatever it takes to find him and those responsible for his disappearance. "

"Thanks, Governor. We appreciate the help."

◆ ◆ ◆

Linda Cunningham paced the floor and wrung her hands; *Ron would have told me if he thought he wasn't going to be home tonight. What on earth has happened to him? It's past midnight.*

"Linda, this is Jim at the jail. I hate like the dickens to have to call you this late, and to the one to tell you this. We found Ron's car out behind the high school. We're afraid he may have been killed."

Linda dropped the phone and fell to the floor.

◆ ◆ ◆

Immediately after the arrests of Rivers and Nona, TBI agent, Danny, tapped Ron on the shoulder. "Hey, Treasury Agent Steve

Warshaw wants to see us back in the other room."

"Ron," Warshaw said, "Danny and I have just talked to Jim Parrott, the agent in charge at Lynchburg. He says it's total chaos up there at your office. Every law enforcement agency for miles around has got somebody there, and all the TV stations and reporters are there asking a lot of questions. We have two options. Number one, we can continue the investigation, and let everyone think you're dead. Or, number two, we can take what we have and shut it down. It's a mess up there. The decision is up to you. Just don't answer their questions, and for God's sake, don't sign anything."

Ron's mind was buzzing like powerful saw, cutting through the rubbish of life. He was certain that others were involved. In his mind, this was far from over! On the trip back to

Lynchburg with agent Wix and Inspector Huckabee, and with Moon sitting next to him in the back seat of the unmarked cruiser, wild thoughts were nagging him. *Will they continue trying to kill me,* he wondered. *What would happen if the investigation were to be called off?* Moon had developed a case relationship with him. He would not be left out of this process if it continued.

While Ron's mind was whirring, flashbacks came to him. First, the attempt to burn the jail went flooding through his consciousness.

Leah was playing in the foyer of the juvenile women's cells. "Daddy," she said, her lower lip protruding, "my crayons are all melting. The floor is hot."

Ron reached down and felt the floor. It was most definitely hot to the touch! He swiftly discovered that there was a fire under the floor. An open hole had been stuffed with papers and clothes, and set on fire. The flames were jumping ever higher! Grabbing a water hose, Ron began dousing the blazes and yelling for someone to call the fire department.

As this remembrance dissolved, Ron closed his eyes, only to be haunted by another dark memory; that of the roadside park incident in which he had been dodging a stream of bullets. Chills crawled up and down his spine as he recalled the flash of light, and the sound of the shots which had nearly hit him.

Then, he thought about Jerry Dean Wade, and the incident in which he had been fired upon from Tanyard Hill. Wade had gone to trial, but received a minimum sentence. *Would they now tie this to Rivers?* Ron laid his head back against the rest, and slowly allowed his eyelids to shut again. This pivotal night had grossly taken its toll on both his acumen and his body.

♦ ♦ ♦

It was 4:00 AM Thursday. Linda's gaunt face lit up like a matchless sunrise. Could it be true? Was her husband still alive? *Thank God!* A bedraggled Ron dashed through the darkness to meet her, throwing his husky arms tightly around her slender, shaking form. But could life ever be the same?

"Sheriff, Jack Blair, Channel 4 News, how do you feel? What caused these people to want to kill you?"

"No comment," Ron grunted, pushing away the prodigious mike which it seemed that Blair was attempting to shove down his throat.

"Sheriff Cunningham, what about a book? Will there be a book in the making soon? I'd like to do the story? How about a movie? This is as good as *Walking Tall*!" This microphone bore a large number 2, and was no more appreciated than the first.

"Listen, I've been advised not to sign anything. There will be a trial. That's all I've got to say for now."

The lot at the Moore County Jail was swarming with news crews and rubber-necking publicity hounds, just as he had been warned. The Tullahoma News, The Nashville Tennessean and Banner, and cameras from the television stations, all begged for the story. The one-traffic-light town which time had forgotten was at the center of the spotlight.

Ron sighed deeply. This was just too much on his family. He knew that he had made the right decision. He would call of the investigation.

Chapter Nineteen

"Earl James, you are under arrest for conspiracy to commit murder and solicitation to take a human life in the case of Sheriff Ron Cunningham. Anything you say..."

"I know my rights, guys." At home in Lynchburg, early that fateful morning, James was just as surprised as had been Clint and Nona Rivers.

"I want to make a deal with you guys." Earl said, as he was being driven to the jail. The look on his face reflected sincere desperation.

"Shut up man, we don't make deals with criminals." Moon spurted out.

"Hey, guys, you might be surprised. I've got something that's hot. I can prove that Governor Ray Blanton is corrupt."

Vince glanced at Earl, then back at Moon. "What the heck are you talking about?"

"Do we have a deal, or not?"

"I told you, we can't promise you anything. What you got for us?"

"I just paid Governor Blanton $15,000 to get my brother out of prison. He got him pardoned."

♦ ♦ ♦

Sheriff Ron Cunningham gritted his teeth and tightened his jaws. "They put me through that for two weeks, and then they let them out!" It seemed that smoke was rising from his head. "Now I'm back in the same spot I was before, only it's worse. My family's worried about it and I'm worried about it, too. They're going to be doubly after me now," Ron told the reporter with the Tennessean, the major newspaper in Nashville, on Thursday February 15th, the next day after returning from the harrowing ordeal in Chattanooga.

What next, Ron wondered. *Who would let these jerks out on bond?*

In the same paper, on Friday, another headline read, "Blanton Aides' Licenses Probe Target."

In 1977, Marie Ragghianti, the head of the Tennessee Board of Pardons and Paroles, had been removed from office after refusing to release prisoners who, it was alleged, had bribed aides to Blanton for their release. Raggianti, a former Florida beauty queen, then a single mother, became known as the whistle-blower, which started the spiral of events leading into the Blanton administration clemency-for-cash scandal. Fred Thompson, then known only for a peripheral role in the Watergate trial, later a well-known actor, and eventually US Senator, defended Raggianti in her landmark case against Blanton's corrupt administration, and won. This being the first time a sitting governor had been brought to trial, the case jump-started his legal and political career.

As previously noted, the governor had just left office early, but not before pardons had been issued to fifty-two felons, including a double-murderer, and James's brother. Members of the governor's staff were convicted, but Blanton himself was never personally charged. The information given to Moon and Joe Vince, however, brought the matter of the Governor's direct involvement to light, which effectively ended his political career. He and his wife, Betty, soon divorced. Both have since passed away.

Wrap Up

The three suspects were held in Moore County until they were extradited to Hamilton County to stand trial. Later, after five attempts for trial dates, Clinton Rivers and Earl James were tried in Hamilton County Criminal Court, and found guilty on charges of solicitation to commit murder in the first degree, and conspiracy to take human life. Both were sentenced to only three years on each of these charges; six years total. These particular charges, however, were dropped against Nona, who was only convicted on the firearms charge, and given a mere sixty days in jail, and a $50 fine.

But the real story is the fact that not only did Earl James negotiate a plea bargain for himself, but also for his co-conspirator, Clinton Rivers. According to Tennessee Code Annotated, 40-35-110, "Felonies are classified, for the purpose of sentencing, into five categories: (1) Class A felonies; (2) Class B felonies; (3) Class C felonies; (4) Class D felonies; (5) Class E felonies." According to 40-35-112, sentence Ranges, the least of these is Range I. These "Ranges" are broken down into the Classes from A to E, above. Based on a recent case in the Tennessee Court of Criminal Appeals held at Knoxville, which I shall not name due to confidentiality, page six of the court records state that solicitation to commit first degree murder is a Class B felony, and carries a lesser sentence than attempted first degree murder. Also under Section 40 of the Tennessee Code, this charge alone carries a minimum sentence for even Range I offenders, of eight years, and as much as twelve years [40-35-112 (a) (2)]. For Range II offenders, this minimum was increased to twelve years, with a maximum of twenty. For Range III, it the minimum is twenty years. And this does not include the other charges of conspiracy and interstate theft.

In a strikingly similar case, though more individuals were targeted, according to a report by Channel 2 news in Nashville on July 14th, 2009, a Putnam County, Tennessee man was sentenced to 325 years in prison for soliciting the murders of a local sheriff's deputy, an agent with the Bureau of Alcohol, Tobacco, Firearms and an informant, in November of 2008.

In this case, the defendant's girlfriend had been selling cocaine to an undercover deputy, and a confidential informant. After the informant died of a drug overdose, the pair decided that if the deputy were killed, there would be no one left to testify against them. They then hired an ATF agent, introduced to them by another informant, as a "hit man", promising him $15,000 to make the hit. They then gave cocaine as a down payment.

The two were arrested the same day. While in custody, awaiting trial, they learned the identity of the second informant and the ATF agent. The man then formulated another plan to have them killed, soliciting a cell mate, promising drugs as payment. He then attempted to put the plot into action by a series of letters sent from prison. In December of 2008, the girlfriend pled guilty to murder for hire, and received only a seventy-five month sentence.

Though infinitely more complex, this case shows how such charges are handled when a plea is not accepted, as opposed to when one is.

Plainly and painfully stated, Earl James's request for a "deal" was most assuredly granted. Information regarding Governor Ray Blanton apparently outranked a conspiracy and solicitation to take the life of a small-town sheriff, even when the highest authorities were involved.

For Ron Cunningham, the effect of these traumatic events would remain an ever-present reality, and serve to shape the remainder of his career, and indeed, his, and his family's very lives. The possible consequences of the early release of James and Rivers threw a devastating blow to the feeling of safety of not only Ron, but of Linda and their children. Nothing could ever give them back the peace which they needed.

Epilogue

Ron Cunningham became so well-known that Jack Daniel Distillery used a photo of him and the jail for an ad in Rolling Stone Magazine (see cover picture).

In 1985, a movie was produced titled **Marie**, in which Fred Thompson played himself, based on a book by Peter Maas, about the Raggianti case. The film also stared Sissy Spacek in the title role, as well as a star-studded cast including Jeff Daniels and Morgan Freeman. The film was directed by Roger Donalson, with a screenplay by John Briley of **Ghandi** fame.

In 1994, a pilot movie was scheduled to be filmed for a TV series about the life of Lacy "Moon" Brown, in which Ron's case was to be the subject. This, however, never reached fruition, in spite of much publicity, due to personal and legal matters regarding the persons involved. This case, nonetheless, made Moon more of a legend than ever.

The story of Ron's ordeal was spread around the country, and considered by Robert "Phil" McCarty to be the "greatest role" of his career, according to an article in his local paper, "The Herald" in June, 1989, entitled, "Unequaled Undercover".

Ron Cunningham accomplished an alarming amount, both as head deputy, and as sheriff, even to getting a bill passed through the Tennessee House and Senate during the 1977 convention. The bill replaced the provision limiting sheriffs to three two year terms with one which allowed Tennessee sheriffs to serve an unlimited number of consecutive four year terms. Though this convention was long, and generally contentious, Ron personally walked the bill through, obtained the signatures of the Governor and the state Comptroller, and got it passed into law in the quickest time of any bill in state history. For this he was issued a special certificate of recognition by J.D. Lee, president of the convention, as an Honorary Delegate.

He was directly responsible for bringing to justice a great number of drug dealers, as well as those responsible for both local and interstate theft, murders, and other crimes. As sheriff he also recaptured escapees from other states and held them for extradition.

Ron's daughters tell him that the best part of their day while growing up was when he came home. His work never kept him from showing them how much they meant to him.

He was the only sheriff of his county to participate in an NWA exhibition match with a heavyweight champion.

Even now, Ron Cunningham, who studied criminal investigation as sheriff, continues to fight for law, order and justice, as an Investigative Captain with the Tullahoma Police Department. He is well respected in the surrounding communities. He is an active member of both Clan Cunningham International, and of the Highland Rim Scottish Society in Tullahoma. He is also the Vice President of the Coffee County Fraternal Order of Police.

Pictorial

Lacy Daniel "Moon" Brown has been called "an undercover legend". His cases, including this one, which he considered among his top stings, have been published in many national publications. Moon died on Friday, October 27, 2006, in Greensboro, NC, at the age of 63. -Photo, property of Ron Cunningham

Joe Vince in 2002 as Chief of Firearms Enforcement Division of ATF, which is under the US Department of Treasury. Joe highly praised Lacy Brown, saying that they had never lost a case in which his expert services were utilized. –Sketch by Stan St. Clair

Port Huron Sergeant Robert "Phil" McCarty, known as "Shooter", was often used when a smooth-talking dope dealer was needed. His cool head was invaluable in this case and many more undercover assignments.
–Photo Times Herald, 1989

A young Ron Cunningham in the Navy in the early 1970's. His Naval service prepared him to be an effective law enforcement officer.
- Photo, property of Ron Cunningham

Ron with 1978 NWA Heavyweight Champion Wrestler, Terry Sawyer, who held an exhibition match with Sheriff Ron Cunningham on July 14, 1978 at 8:30 at Moore County High School, where Ron left his car the night he was to have been killed in February, 1979.
-Photo, property of Ron Cunningham

Former location of the White Rabbit Saloon, now a hardware and general store.
- Photo, St. Clair

Moore County Courthouse, built in the 1880's
-Photo, St. Clair

Bridge on Hwy. 55, near high school, under
Which Ron foubd stolen items from Co-op.
- Photo, St. Clair

Former location of "C&N Plaza". Current
name b locked out for privacy.
- Photo, St. Clair

Former location of the mobile home around which the motorcycle incident occurred while Ron was a deputy.
- Photo, St. Clair

Redd's Grocery to which Ron was called at the time of the motorcycle incident.
- Photo, St. Clair

Moore County Jail where Ron and family lived during his tenure as Sheriff. They were the last family to occupy this facility as a home. The jail is now a museum.
- Photo, St. Clair

Former location of the roadside park to which Ron was called, and where he was fired upon.
- Photo, St. Clair

Former location of the shed in which "Tanner Jackson" was murdered. The old barns here are a county landmark.
- Photo, St. Clair

229

The spot behind Moore County High School where Ron parked his car the night of his proposed murder. The school is still functional in this location.
- Photo, St. Clair

The alley where Ron was standing when he was fired upon from Tanyard Hill, seen in the distance, here.
- Photo, St. Clair

This is a portion of a 1986 autographed handbill promoting Ron Cunningham in a new bid for the office of Sheriff of Moore County.
–Photo property of Ron Cunningham

Leonard Ray Blanton as Governor of Tennessee (1-18-1975 to 1-16-1979). Though never convicted on the charge of selling the pardons, he was found guilty on charges of selling liquor licenses, and served time in the federal penitentiary. He died on November 22, 1996.
– Photo, Public Domain

Ron in his Cunningham Kilt – Photo property of Ron Cunningham

Cunningham History

As a member of Clan Cunningham International, Ron has a keen interest in the history of his family, and how he came to be a native of middle Tennessee.

The name Cunningham, which is said to signify "courage in battle", may have been derived from "Cunedda" who was a king of the "Gododdin", a celtic branch of Britons called by the Romans, "Votadini", according to Clan Cunningham historians. Dalriada was an ancient kingdom which occupied the area now known as Ireland. When these peoples emigrated to modern day Scotland in circa 500 AD, they were confronted by the Strathelyde and Gododdin Brittons and Picts. The name

Cunedda eventually evolved into words like Cyning, Kynge, and finally, King. The "ham" signifies "hamlet" and was likely added by the Normans after their invasion in 1066. Others claim that in the Celtic tongue, Cunedda was rendered as Cinneidigh, which meant "ugly", or "grim-headed". The name gradually became associated with the district of Carrick in Ayrshire, Scotland.

On a recent trip to the mother country, in a visit to Ayrshire, Ron did research on his ancestors, and put it together with fragments which were already known to him.

The word "cunning" may mean "coney", or rabbit, according to some. This theory gained popularity because the coat of arms of the Earls of Glencairn reflects two coneys as supporters. Another interesting note is the fact that in a Gaelic on-line dictionary, the word "coney", for rabbit, translates as "coinean", and the name Cunningham translates as "coineagan".

The earliest known in the Cunningham line was Warnebald, a vassal under Hugh de Morville, constable of Scotland, about the middle of the twelfth century. De Morville granted him land known as Cunninghame in the vicinity of Kilmaurs. The name Warnebale is evidently Gothic, and may indicate that he was of Danish descent. No surname is indicated for Warnebald.

Robert de Cunninghame de Kilmaurs, the first known to bear the "de Cunningham" title or name, gave the patronage of the church at Kilmaurs to the Abbey of Kebo. He was succeeded by his son, who bore the same name, and was made Lord of Kilmaurs. He had three sons. The eldest, another Robert, was his heir. From there the succession was as follows:

Harvey de Cunyngham of Kilmaurs

Sir William Cunyngjame

Edward Cunynghame (his son, Richard was the ancestor of the Cunninghams of Polmaise, who are now not known by that name).

Gilbert Cunynghame of Kilmaurs – one of Robert Bruce's nominees in the competition with Balliol.

Sir Robert Cunynghame of Kilmaurs, who originally swore the family's allegiance to Edward I, but later joined with Bruce, and was rewarded by him with valuable lands in Kilmaurs, part of the spoils of the Balliol party.

Sir William Cuninghame of Kilmaurs, who married Eleanor Bruce, Countess of Carrick, and was created Earl of Carrick, though his only issue was by a former marriage.

Sir William Cuninghame of Kilmaurs, who acquired a great addition to the family estate by marriage to Margaret, the eldest co-heir of Sir Robert Danielstoun. His part of the vast property was the baronies of Danielstoun and Finlaystoun in Renfrewshire; Kilmarnock, in Danbartonshire; Redhall and Colintoun in Midlothian; together with Glencairn, in Dumfrieshire, afterwards the chief title of the family.

Sir Robert Cuninghame of Kilmaurs (15th century). He was succeded by his eldest son, Alexander, the first Earl of Glencairn.

The Earls of Glencairn were, in chronological order:

1st Earl, Alexander Cunninghame – 1488
   (killed in battle)

2nd Earl, Robert Cunninghame – 1488-1503

3rd Earl, Cuthbert Cunninghame – 1503-1540

4th Earl, William Cunninghame – 1540-1547

5th Earl, Alexander Cun ninghame – 1547-1574

6th Earl, William Cunninghame – 1574-1581

7th Earl, James Cunninghame – 1581-1629

8th Earl, William Cunninghame – 1629-1631

9th Earl, William Cunninghame – 1631-1664

10th Earl, Alexander Cunninghame – 1664-1670

11th Earl, John Cunninghame – 1670-1703

12th Earl, William Cunninghame – 1703-1734

13th Earl, William Cunninghame – 1734-1775

14th Earl, James Cunninghame – 1775-1791

15th Earl, John Cunninghame – 1791-1706

John was the brother of the 14th Earl, James. Since there was no heir, the Earldom has since remained vacant.

CUNNINGHAM VOYAGE TO AMERICA

Ron's ancestor, Joseph Cunningham, was born in Ayrshire in about 1680, and married a local lady named Mary, about three years his junior, about the turn of the eighteenth century. Joseph and Mary immigrated to the Virginia Colony, and followed the Wilderness Road along the scenic Blue Ridge Mountains into Rowan County, North Carolina.

There, they gave birth to their son, Joseph the younger, about 1738. It was here that Mary and Joseph, Sr., died. Joseph II married Ann Bunt, and moved to Rockingham County, NC. They continued the tradition of the name Joseph for a son who would be Ron's ancestor. Joseph III and his wife, Jane, gave birth to Joseph IV, who married Elizabeth Simpson on 13 April, 1793. This couple pressed forward into the state of Tennessee, following the beautiful landscape along the Clinch River, stopping in Roane County, where there son Richard, was born on 10 November 1803. Then, they continued across the Cumberland Mountains, through Crab Orchard, eventually settling in Warren County, originally including what is now Coffee, Cannon, Van Buren, and Grundy Counties, near the present Coffee County line.

Richard married Mary "Polly" Bickle. They became the parents of William on 19 June 1829, who married Sarah Banks in what was, by that time, Coffee County on 20 March 1853. On 12 February 1900, William died Coffee County.

Richard and other family members are buried at Viola, Tennessee. The family is prominent in the area of Warren, Coffee and Moore Counties.

The Cunningham-Gribble Cemetery, near Rock Island State Park in Warren County, contains the graves of relatives

Bibliography

The Nashville Banner, Nashville, TN
Thursday afternoon, February 15, 1979,
pp 1 & 4

The Tennessean, Nashville, TN
Friday, February 16, 1979, pp 1 & 4

The Tullahoma News, Tullahoma, TN
Friday morning, February 16, 1979, pp 1A, 2A

Rolling Stone Magazine, New York, NY
April 12, 1980, p 57

The Detroit Free Press Magazine, Detroit, MI
January 27, 1991, cover story, "Phases of the
Moon", p 5

The Times Herald, Port Huron, MI
Sunday June 14, 1989 Section B, pp 1 & 2B

News and Record, Greensboro, NC
Tuesday, October 31, 2006, p B4

County News Weekly, Winchester, TN
November 21, 1994, pp 1 & 5

PBS, Online Newsletter, Tracking Firearms
http://www.pbs.org/newshour/bb/law/july-dec02/ballistics_10-18.html

World of Wrestling, On Line Profiles
http://www.onlineworldofwrestling.com/profiles/t/terry-sawyer.html

Official wire and phone-tap records and transcripts in the possession of Captain Ron Cunningham

Tennessee Code Annotated 40-35-110, 40-35-112

Wikipedia articles on Marie Raggianti at http://en.wikipedia.org/wiki/Marie_Ragghianti and the movie Marie at http://en.wikipedia.org/wiki/Marie_(film)

Wikipedia article on the Tennessee Constitution at http://en.wikipedia.org/wiki/Tennessee_State_Constitution section on the 1977 Convention and its Aftermath

Material belonging Lester Brown which was to be used in the making of the TV movie pilot for the proposed series entitled "The Adventures of an Undercover Legend", featuring the Ron Cunningham case.

Honorary Delegate Certificate from State of Tennessee, 1977 Legislative Convention, property of Ron Cunningham.

WKRN, Channel 2, News Story, July 14, 2009, http://www.wkrn.com/Global/story.asp?S=1 0725818 "Baxter Man Receives 325-Year Prison Sentence".

Clan Cunningham Society, USA official website located at:

www.clancunninghamusa.org/history.htm

About the Author

Stan St. Clair is a semi-retired insurance agent and manager, who for a number of years operated American Benefit Services, an interstate final expense insurance agency in the U.S. He is also the owner of St. Clair Publications, which may be found on-line at http://stan.stclair.net. In 2009, he began offering publishing services to other authors, providing a showcase for their work.

Stan is the author of six other published books to date. His nostalgic poetry has been published locally, nationally, and inter-nationally in newspapers, magazines, and books. In 2004 he was recognized in *The International Who's Who in Poetry*, and was featured in their annual publication (Waterman Press, Owings Mills, Maryland, USA). He was also selected for inclusion in the 2007-2008 *Cambridge Who's Who Among Executives and Professional, Honors Edition.*

He holds a professional designation of L.U.T.C.F., and has degrees in Religious Education and Sacred Literature from Covington College and Theological Seminary in Rossville, Georgia, a suburb of Chattanooga, Tennessee.

Stan has been an officer of the Scottish Clan Sinclair Association, U.S.A since early in 2002, and was the 2006 and 2007 Eastern Regional Vice President. He co-founded the worldwide Sinclair DNA Project with distant cousin, Steve St. Clair, which compares YDNA of Sinclairs and St. Clairs at www.stclairresearch.com. He has been a regular writer for his official clan association publication, *Yours Aye*, for a number of years, and his articles have been published in several countries. In 2003, he was knighted by the S.M.O.T.J. as a Knight Templar, in which he is currently inactive.

He is past president of his local Kiwanis Club, of which he is a charter member, and has served in every office of the club. He and his lovely wife, Rhonda, have traveled extensively to many exotic spots, across the U.S., and in numerous other countries.

Both Stan and Rhonda are active members of the Cumberland Presbyterian Church, and live in McMinnville, Tennessee. Stan has four children, one step-daughter, and fourteen grandchildren.

The End

Made in the USA
Lexington, KY
20 April 2012